Fr...
GREEN RIVER
to the
Lily of the Valley

the
Susie Manns
story

From the
GREEN RIVER
to the
Lily of the Valley

the
Susie Manns
story

Susie Manns-Bates

HUNTER ENTERTAINMENT NETWORK
Colorado Springs, Colorado

To order products, or for any other correspondence:

Hunter Entertainment Network
Colorado Springs, Colorado 80840
www.hunter-ent-net.com
Tel. (253) 906-2160
E-mail: contact@hunter-entertainment.com
Or reach us on Facebook at: Hunter Entertainment Network
"Offering God's Heart to a Dying World"

This book and all other Hunter Entertainment Network™ Hunter Heart Publishing™, and Hunter Heart Kids™ books are available at Christian bookstores and distributors worldwide.

Chief Editor: Deborah G. Hunter
Book cover design: Phil Coles Independent Design
Layout & logos: Exousia Marketing Group www.exousiamg.com
ISBN (Hardcover): 978-1-937741-13-6
ISBN (Paperback): 978-1-937741-01-3
ASIN (eBook) : B0CJGYN7QC
Printed in the United States of America.

Dedication

I dedicate this book to every sinner like me that needs to hear the truth and to know the saving grace of Jesus Christ, Romans 10:9-10.

Acknowledgments

I would like to acknowledge first and foremost Jesus Christ who is God, for saving me and restoring my life for HIS Glory and my Good. I would like to thank my husband, Toney for always bringing me closer to Jesus Christ. I want to thank, Barbara Bennett & Jean (who is with Jesus), for helping get me free of prostitution. I would like to thank Jody Davis, for *Up and Out*. I would like to thank Alcoholics Anonymous for my early sobriety. I would like to thank Dani Collins, Anna Elzinga, Robyn Wiebe, Cathy Davis, Amanda, and so many more that counseled me through my recovery and still stand by me today. I would like to thank my loyal friends who for years have stood by me, Teresa Smiley, Julia Laranang, Rosemary Funk, David Bevers, and so many others who have listened to me when I was down. I would like to thank my Pastors and Elders who helped me learn and grow in Jesus Christ: Pastor Jeff Moorehead, Pastor Russ Williams, Dr. Andre Sims, Pastor Bob Faulk, Dr. Grady Smith, Elder Stephen McNeal, Pastor K.C. Cook, Pastor Floyd Earlywine, and so many others that have sown into my Christian walk.

I would like to thank Deborah Hunter, my book publisher, for hearing the call of GOD to write stories of HIS glory. I would like to thank Deborah for her patience as I wrote this very difficult life story and her encouragement and Bible knowledge to enhance a wonderful story for the Lord Jesus Christ.

I would like to acknowledge each and every one of my biological family members, who grew up in the same trauma as me and are living proof that God is real. Who forgave me and reconciled with me when I needed to know that God was real in reconciliation. I love them each dearly and pray that they all come to the saving Grace and Truth of our Lord and Savior, Jesus Christ who is Himself God.

Last, but certainly not least, I would like to thank my children and grandchildren, who make me cry at the thought of them. I love them so dearly and each one of them played a big part in my life and in this book. I pray that each one of you learn that there is only one way to peace and that is through the Love of Jesus Christ. The world can offer you nothing more than "a pipe dream with melted ice cream," but Jesus offers you Eternal Life. You have been the reason I have fought to live my life, and I will continue to fight until the day Jesus comes to get me. I love you all so very much, *Mama & Grandma*.

Foreword

I first heard Susie Mann's voice over the telephone sometime in May of 2010, just as I was taking over of the women's ministry office in the church I was attending at the time, *Christ's Church* in Federal Way, WA. Her voice was full of enthusiasm, as she spoke for the homeless shelter she was working for in Tacoma at the time. She wanted to know how our church could help her in ministering to some of the women. I didn't know. I immediately summoned Dani Collins, who was just stepping down from her former women's ministry director job. Her eyes lit up and she said, "Yes, I know Susie, let's help her!" Dani coordinated help for Susie and her ministry and soon afterwards, I started seeing Susie at church and began getting to know her more. We ended up in a Bible study together and I knew immediately that this woman of God had a story. Susie attended our church until she and her husband, Toney started their own church and ministry. At that point, I still hadn't heard her full story, just bits of it from our women's care team visits and I knew I wanted to know more.

Fast forward a few years until May of 2018. As I was just leaving my women's ministry job and from being on staff at *Christ's Church*, I got a call from Susie. She was lonely and suffering from fear and anxiety again, unable to leave her home and was reaching out for help as she knew isolating was not good for her walk with God. Some of her past's traumas and sorrows were creeping up again even after being saved and living for God for many years.

There was no doubt God wanted me to counsel, encourage, and support Susie. That very Saturday, I went to her house to visit and haven't left since. Almost Every Saturday for over four years, we spent digging into the Word of God, praying, counseling, and encouraging each other. I was to be "her counselor," but I left many times being humbled and inspired myself as I gradually heard Susie's story, how God had so miraculously saved her, both physically and spiritually. A true friendship began to grow as we have now walked together as sisters in the Lord for over six years.

As I see the ministry that God has given Susie and her husband Toney, I marvel at God's equipping of this passionate, joyful, humble servant of God. She (and all of us) are not without our issues. Seeing how God has displayed His Grace in Susie's life in spite of her many physical, and emotional challenges, is truly a testimony of God's sanctifying love and grace!

Her love and passion for the "least of these," the homeless, addicted, and hurting men and women come directly from *her story*. As sad as it is, she has chosen to comfort and love those as she herself has been loved and comforted by our Living Savior! God has redeemed her lost years and now given her a fervor, and joyful eagerness to share the love of God with everyone!

Anna Elzinga
Friend and Biblical Counselor

Table of Contents

Introduction

E ach of us on the face of this Earth will go through tests, trials, and tribulations throughout our lives. Some maybe more than others, but each of our walks is unique and predestined by our Father in Heaven. He knows the struggles and the triumphs of each of His children, and though we may not see it as we are going through them, He walks alongside of us every step of the way until we accept and acknowledge His Son, Jesus Christ, as our Lord and Savior. I knew of God growing up, but it was, indeed, a surface-level "knowing," not a strong, intimate relationship with the God of Heaven and Earth. Though I didn't have this kind of intimacy with God, deep down I knew somehow, He was with me.

Through all of the ups and downs, trauma and turmoil, in my life, I seemed to find Him at every crossroad. It was if He was silently walking with me, granting me His strength to carry on, when I thought there was nothing left within me to go on. The title of my book, "From the Green River to the Lily of the Valley," is my life's story chronicling the journey from death to life and every facet of my life in between. Though traumatic and full of chaos from some of my earliest childhood memories, it is, indeed, *my story* and one God has used to bring me out of the darkness and into His marvelous light. It is my testimony of His love, forgiveness, compassion, patience, and sovereignty in my life.

"No one has ever seen God, but the one and only Son, who is himself God and is in closest relationship with the Father, has made him known" John 1:18, NIV.

My journey has been a very difficult and challenging one, and one many would choose rather not to write about, but I am compelled by the love and freedom that God has brought into my life to share boldly and transparently, so that others can also experience that divine touch from the Father in Heaven. The times we are living in are very dark and many are walking the streets of America, and around the world, bound in chains desperately seeking a way out. Some make it out, but many do not and I have witnessed this with my own eyes. I walked those lonely streets and lived in utter darkness, an empty shell simply existing in this world, but not living … truly living a life of freedom.

As long as I have breath in my body, I will shout of His goodness to all those that will hear of the One that touched and saved my soul, and delivered me from the destruction mapped out for my life here in this world. He snatched me out of the grips of hell and translated me into His heavenly Kingdom, offering me a seat in the heavenly places with Christ, His Son, as an heir. Susie Brady … an alcoholic, a drug addict, a prostitute, a gambler, and as Paul stated, "the chief of sinners," God made an heir with His Precious and Holy Son, Jesus. My friend, no matter what "label" has been stamped upon you in this life, I am here as a witness to let you know that you no longer have to carry that *scarlet letter* upon your chest. You do not have to be marked for the rest of your life as an outcast in this world; there is a loving, caring Father in Heaven that is ready to change your name, your location, and your story. He will not erase your story, but He will use it for His Glory! He specializes in turning broken things into magnificent vessels. He majors in turning what the devil meant for harm around for His ultimate glory and our undesevering good.

"From the Green River to the Lily of the Valley" is a roller coaster ride that is sure to make you cry, laugh, get angry, rejoice, and simply thank God for His hand of healing, deliverance, and freedom. It will have you on the edge of your seat, especially if you have walked through some of the things I have in my life or you know of someone who has, or is currently. There are many of us out there wandering in the darkness, seeking to find some sort of connection in this world, some inkling of purpose for living. Be extremely careful not to judge others as you do not know the trauma and torment many of these people have walked through in their lives. So many have been broken, abused, and traumatized throughout their lives, and they simply need someone to see them, to hear them, to love them. Choose to be a light in this dark world, a hand of compassion, a healing balm that God can use to bring His children back home into His loving arms.

"He said to his disciples, "The harvest is great, but the workers are few. So pray to the Lord who is in charge of the harvest; ask him to send more workers into his fields" Matthew 9:37-38, NKJV.

Chapter 1

We are All Born into Sin

"... for all have sinned and fall short of the glory of God."
Romans 3:23, NKJV

M y name is Susie, and I was born on August 17th, 1962, to Thomas and Irene Brady in Portland, Oregon. I had six brothers and sisters, and I was the second to the youngest. I did not realize until I was about 2 ½ years old that I was born into a very chaotic family. I was very smart as early on as I can remember. I had a good memory, and I would sing at the kitchen table from around two or three years old. I loved the attention of my family, and I loved having a big family. We learned how to stick together very early on in life because of our father's addiction to alcoholism. My father was a truck driver for Chevron, and he drank every single day of his life that I can remember, up until I was around the age of eleven or twelve. His addiction nightmare ended regarding active addiction when I was thirteen years old. Subsequently, my pain began to manifest, which would take a lifetime to heal.

My father was a blackout drunk; he would curse all night, yelling and screaming. I don't know what he did to my mother, but she screamed almost every night of the week. He never left her alone. The poor woman never got any sleep and she worked tirelessly every day to take care of us kids. She was a good mom. My father went to work every day; he did not miss work often. I guess you could say he was a "functioning alcoholic". He was extremely detached from emotions and incredibly broken himself. It was just a tremendously hard childhood for us.

"For wherever there is jealousy and selfish ambition, there you will find disorder and evil of every kind" James 3:16, NLT.

We don't fully understand the consequences of the choices we make in our lives, whether by consent or through generational curses passed down through our families, and how it will affect our lives, our marriages, and our children. Whatever had taken place in my father's childhood was now having a direct effect on our family. His alcoholism was not the root, but a branch. We must always search for the root in order to expose and subsequently reveal why we do the things we do.

By the time I was five years old, I had become very close to my older brother, my only brother Michael. He was about 12 ½ years older than me. He was seventeen years old when I was five. Apparently, he had gone to seminary, and I believe something either happened to him there, or something took place at home. We were Catholic kids who went to Catholic schools. Catechism was our entire life. My brother was becoming a priest, and I remember when he came home, he got a job at a burger restaurant on Killingsworth and Williams Avenue in northeast Portland. He would buy me gifts and bought me a teapot, table and chairs, and cute little outfits. I felt very close to him as he would protect me from my father, or at least I thought he would. I was very scared of my father and the trauma that was taking place in our home. I just didn't understand what was going on. My older sisters, who were twins, were always protecting us. They were seven years older than me. They had to be adults when my poor mother had no strength left to fight.

"Such love has no fear, because perfect love expels all fear. If we are afraid, it is for fear of punishment, and this shows that we have not fully experienced his perfect love" 1 John 4:18, NLT.

My life was centered around fear. At every turn, it reared its ugly head in my life. Just as the scripture states, *"... there is no fear in love,"* but though I had both of my parents and we were taken care of financially, I do not believe any of us knew what true love meant. Not my father, not my mother, and I was certainly heading down a destructive path that was sure to taint and pervert the meaning of authentic love in my life. I believed our dad loved us in his own way, but somewhere in his life, love was perverted for him. Our mother loved us dearly, but her experience with my father was toxic, traumatic, and tormenting for her. There was no way we could escape the effects of this toxicity in their marriage, as it trickled down upon us children.

My oldest sister was in the nunnery, at that time, so I really didn't get to see her much. My baby sister slept in the room with me, and I had to protect her at night from my father, and from her fear of hearing my mother scream every night. I can still remember so clearly what she sounded like, and it breaks my heart to this day. She would wake up so tired every morning and had really dark circles under her eyes. She was absolutely exhausted and because she was so abused, she was not able to think correctly. My mother always tried to protect us and made sure we were always cared for, sending us to the best schools. I don't know how she was even able to afford these schools. My father used to always gamble and drink and squander his paycheck, so she would have to make ends meet. She would work at our school to help with our tuition; she was just a really good woman.

"Train up a child in the way he should go, And when he is old he will not depart from it." Proverbs 22:6

My mother was raised Protestant and became a Catholic when she married my father. She was saved at an early age on April 7, 1947, truly. But unfortunately, a broken woman of God. One thing about my mother was that she could keep secrets really well. She held inside all that was going on in her life and in our home. I can only imagine how she felt and all that was going through her mind, let alone continuing to be a wife to her abusive husband, my father, and gracefully taking care of me and my siblings, as well as her home. There are no words that can adequately describe the woman I called "Mama".

I am not fully sure of my mother's upbringing, but simply from her demeanor, you knew that she had some sort of relationship with God. She had to have considered the pure strength and commitment to remain in such a chaotic marriage and honor her husband, my dad, the way she did. There is much to be said about a woman that can endure such suffering yet still raise her children and continue to instill love and compassion into her children, as well as others. Now, I am not condoning or encouraging women to remain in physically abusive relationships; I am simply revealing the character of my mother, which probably stemmed from many nights of prayer to God. Something, or someone, was providing her the strength to carry on. My fears for her, as well as for us children, were comforted somewhat by her willingness to continue *being Mama*. There were others that provided a sense of normalcy from the abuse, or so I thought.

I saw my brother as my protector, someone who could keep me safe from my father and bring some sort of peace to my heart. He would sit on the couch with me when my father was raging and calm me down. Unfortunately, he used to snort airplane glue and listen to Jefferson Airplane on full blast up in his bedroom. It always made my dad very angry. I remember one day when my dad came home from work and my brother had drug mud in from the outside on his feet, dirtying the carpet with his boots. He was being rebellious against my father, and I honestly do not remember what started the fight, but I recall my father punching him full-fledged in the face like a man. My brother was yelling at him, and my father told him he had to leave our home. I was so terrified! I had a secret that I had not told anyone.

"God would surely have known it, for he knows the secrets of every heart" Psalm 44:21, NLT.

One day before Dad kicked Michael out of the house, in my brand-new robe that my mother had made me for Christmas, my brother walked me down into our basement and put me on the little table he had bought me. I cannot remember exactly what he did to me, but it was something inappropriately sexual. I was very young, so the memory is extremely vague. I know it was my brother and I have gone through a lot of therapy in my life surrounding this sexual abuse. As I stated earlier, I am not sure if something like this had happened to him in seminary, or if it took place in our home. Though this happened to me, I was devastated that he was leaving, as he was my only real protection against my father.

I didn't know Jesus; I did not know God at this time. All I knew is I was all alone in a place that terrified me every single day, and I wasn't sure where to turn for safety.

This was a moment of abandonment for me, as he never came back for me. I was sure he would come back for me because I was so scared, but I never saw him again until I was in my twenties. By this time, he was verbally abusive toward me. He called me a "nigger-lover" because I had brown children. He never once apologized for what he did to me as a child, or how he left me. He never once said, "I'm sorry" for me feeling abandoned and alone my entire childhood. His leaving began a progression of things going wrong in my childhood. Not only did he leave, but my oldest sister left the house, as well. It was now just me, my baby sister, and my twin sisters.

My sisters were my pride and joy as a little girl. I was so proud to be a Brady girl. When I went to school and realized that I was Chris, Karen, Kathy, and Jenny's sister, I felt a part of an unbreakable family. I felt secure and like I would never be alone. My sisters were all their own people with colorful gifts and great personalities. Like all sisters, we fought, we played, and we stuck together. In our family, we also had to survive during horrible times of trauma. Each of us had the same secret that was very hard to keep at times. Especially when our father stood outside intoxicated on most nights screaming racial slurs and abusive innuendos to our African American neighbors. My sisters and I took the brunt end of these racial slurs every time we walked to school and our neighbors let their Doberman pinchers out on us, or when we went to the berry bus and the kids knew who we were and set my sister's hair on fire. The retaliation for his sins were our cross to bear on most days, but we did, and we survived.

From the Green River to the Lily of the Valley

My baby sister was three years younger than me and my best friend for eighteen years. I loved her very much and we spent many days together. We used to soothe each other to sleep at night by massaging each other's faces, when our father was raging in the living room. Jenny took my place as the baby, which was hard at first, but she was so adorable; I loved having a baby sister. We grew up in that home together with different experiences, but we grew up together. Jenny was very compassionate and kind and was always there for me as my life fell apart. As teens, we loved going to scary movies, it was fun when I first got sober. When my first son was born, she was very kind to me and always listened to me. We lost touch for nearly twenty-five years, and it was very hard in all my trauma to not have my sweet baby sister as my friend.

My twin sisters are six years older than me. Everyone loves my twin sisters; they are very popular. They had lots of friends, and I was always so proud when people would say, "Are you their sister?" They helped protect us from our dad's rage and protected my mom from his abuse. They helped with homework and encouraged me. They helped me with sports and everything I needed as a child. I adored them and always looked up to their strength and intelligence. They light up a room when they come in it. I love them dearly. We also lost touch for twenty-five years and it was very hard to not have them in my life. Gratefully, they are in my life now and I am eternally thankful to Jesus for restoring all my siblings to me.

My brother was twelve years older than me. He was a fleeting experience in my life that created lifelong destruction. He was rebellious and on drugs, but he stood up to my dad and it made me feel protected. After he hurt me and left home, I didn't see him until I was in my twenties where he wanted nothing to do with me because of my children. He was strung out on drugs at this point in his life, fighting the fight of recovery. He lost his battle with his recovery when he was 38, and I was 26. He died at the Union Gospel Mission program of a drug overdose. That would linger in my heart and mind for many years to come.

My oldest sister is thirteen years older than I; she babysat me and my baby sister all the time when we were little. She was very tall and beautiful. She had the most beautiful blonde hair. She was very smart, and she was living in the nunnery learning how to become a Catholic nun. After her four years, she decided she wanted to be a lay person and married a wonderful man. She had a great job and she graduated Magna Cum Laude from multiple Master's programs. I was so impressed with how smart and kind she is. I didn't see her for several years and in my adult years, she came back into my life when I had little family contact and supported me in my recovery during very difficult situations. She talked to me on the phone and helped me feel connected to my family when I felt all alone in the world. My life was very chaotic and I understood why no one would want to be in my life, but she was very kind to me during those times of my life and I am eternally grateful for her love and friendship in a time when I was so very alone. I love you honey, forever.

It is interesting that as adults, each one of my siblings has a different perception of what went on in that house. If my siblings are reading this book, I know your memories may be different than mine and I honor the trauma you went through, and I have prayed for you and your healing my entire adult life. I pray you have found Jesus to heal from this very confusing, abusing childhood we lived through. I love you all very much, thank you for all you did to help me survive... Susie.

From the Green River to the Lily of the Valley

I had such a spirit of fear and anxiety from as early on as I can remember. I was terrified of everything, and I was so claustrophobic in my bedroom. My younger sister and I slept in the back bedroom close to our parents. There was no exit, other than the windows. At night, I would sleepwalk in my underwear around the ages of five to seven years old. I would crawl out of the window and walk down to the corner store, Anderson's Corner store, or *Anderson's Grocery Store*. I would go to get my father a newspaper because I thought by doing so that it would make him love me. I thought this might get him to stop doing what he was doing to us in our home, I thought somehow it was my fault he was drinking and maybe I could help him stop. It was horrible the things he did to us and my mother. Neighbors would bring me home around 4:30-5:00am in the morning to my Mama and say, "We found Susie walking in her underwear in the neighborhood." Thank God no one snatched me or took me away. I don't remember much of it because I was so little and I was asleep, but my mother shared with me what took place during that time later on in my life.

One night my baby sister and I were sleeping, and I heard a noise in the backyard. Dad wasn't cursing in the house, so I wondered if he was asleep. I looked out into our backyard and there was a big tree by my window. I saw men chanting and moving in a circle. I immediately jumped back and it scared me. I thought they were devil worshippers or bad people who came to kill us. I was about five or six years old. I didn't know what to do. I ran back to my bed and all the lights in the house were out. So, I ran in my mom's room and went to sleep behind her door. I could hide there and my dad didn't know I was there. Later in life, I would find out those men were the KKK.

For years, I used to be really mad at my mom because no one shared with the doctor what happened to me as a child. I felt betrayed because I was not protected as I should have been, but I realize she did protect us in a way by being a doormat for my father's abuse. She did absolutely cook and clean for us, so she was a mother in those aspects. She also took us to the dentist and to the doctor, as I recall, but she would never tell anyone the trauma we were living in within our home. My grandparents did have money and homes. My grandfather had properties. If she would have told them, I am sure we could have left my dad and moved into one of the properties my grandfather owned, but she kept it all a secret. We could have left and at least given him an opportunity to get help and get better. I did, however, forgive my mother later on in life when I myself became a battered woman, an alcoholic, and a terrible sinner.

"But if you refuse to forgive others, your Father will not forgive your sins" Matthew 6:15, NLT.

My mother became a very bitter woman due to the abuse she suffered at my father's hands. Though he was able to get sober and stop the abuse, it stayed with her all her life. I believe my mother had other mental health issues that we never completely found out concerning her. Even though she suffered through all of this, I know for sure that she loved God and loved her children and her family. For this, I will always be eternally grateful. My mother would always sew Barbie clothes for us for our birthdays. She would buy us the brand-new Barbie and then make the clothes for the dolls. She would always get us things that other kids didn't have. She wanted to make sure that her kids were well taken care of and happy. My mother would "home sew" all of our clothes with the exception of our school uniforms. She was a very domestic woman. She would make homemade jellies and jams, bread, and noodles. Also, homemade pies and cookies.

From the Green River to the Lily of the Valley

My mom was just an incredibly good mother, even though she did not have a lot to go on for all those years. Literally, every single day of her life, she knew her husband was going to come home drunk. It wasn't if, it was when. She somehow dealt with it. It wasn't discussed with a lot of people. I would hear her on the phone discussing it, and she probably confided in one or two people, though I don't know who they were. She was just not in a good place to communicate, which is absolutely understandable for someone that is being abused. I grieve that she had to endure such trauma and turmoil in her life. I now understand that same sin of false pride my mother had, I acquired, and it would severely affect my children in the future.

My mother took all of us to the Catholic church every Sunday. She would wrap all our hair in curlers on Saturday night and we would have burgers for dinner. I loved Saturdays and this ritual to get ready for church. We usually went to the early service, so we could get home for the football game for our Dad. Dad came with us to church even if he was still drunk from the night before. We sat all eight of us like the Brady bunch pretending life was good, while we listened to the Priest share the sermon.

One Sunday on Christmas Eve, we all went to midnight mass, I was anxious about Santa coming that night and I was rolling on the floor under my eldest sister. She had my arm, until I broke free. I saw the live nativity scene on the stage and they said baby Jesus was there. I broke running up the aisle and made it to the manger before the priest could come down the aisle. I picked up what I thought was baby Jesus to only find out it was a doll. I said to the congregation, "Don't worry, it's not Jesus; it's just a doll." This was a theme regarding my faith that would live with me until a great spiritual awakening took place in my life much later.

I had neighbor friends that were special to me, I never thought the other kids liked me, so I worked really hard to keep their friendships. I felt unlovable most of the time. I didn't realize that the sexual abuse I experienced had affected me until I went to the neighbors one day and told all the girls what happened to me. One of the girls went back and told my mom on me and I got in big trouble, and she told me that it was bad to talk that way. So, I never told another person until I was much older about the sexual abuse I suffered by my brother.

One of my neighbor's mom's understood the trauma going on in my house and would listen to me every day and spend time with me and her kids telling stories and cooking for us. She was a wonderful woman, her name was Sharon. She comforted me all the time. I would love sitting on their back patio with her and her children, and I felt a part of the family. She became an advocate for the black and white community to negotiate on police matters. She was a very kind and loving woman. She was one of the first *Angels* God brought in my life to cope with what was going to be a horrific life.

I had another family in the neighborhood that took pity on me because of the family I lived with. They had a St. Bernard and a pool. Their dad must have made super good money, because they had all the things I wished we had in our family. Their daughter Jill and I had been swimming in their pool one Mother's Day. It was one of the only happy places I had in my life at this time. Jill and I would play monopoly and her mom would pretend the kitchen was an ice cream shop and we would get ice cream treats. The only drawback is they had a 150lb. St. Bernard that I was terrified of. So, on this Mother's Day, I decided to muster up enough courage to pet the dog, her name was Sheila; she pummeled me to the ground and stood over me, biting me slightly inches under my eye and inside my mouth. The only thing that saved my life was that the father was outside and he began beating her with a boot.

I walked home in shock bleeding from my eye and mouth. I walked in my parents' house and my mom was panicking when she saw me and my dad said, "Why would you do this to your mom on Mother's Day?" I was too shocked to even pay attention to my dad. My parents rushed me to the ER where I proceeded to tell the surgeon stories while he stitched me up. It helped me feel in control and get through my anxiety. Talking and telling stories was how I learned to cope with all the stresses from then on. I was terrified of dogs from that point forward and never had a dog in my life until forty years later.

Not long after my brother left home, I began to compulsively overeat. In the second grade, I learned what it means to be bullied... I was overweight, so my name changed from Susie to *Bessie the Cow*. They called me many horrible names. Food became even more of my best friend. The only thing I liked about me was my hair. So, I made my mother make sure my hair was perfect when I went to school, hoping this would stop kids from making fun of me. I also learned that if you "buy" your friends, they will like you at least for a while. So, I would take kids to the Dairy Queen and buy French fries for them so they would like me. This became a pattern my entire life beginning at this age.

My mother would have to lock the food up because we simply did not have enough. My father got paid every Thursday, but due to his drinking and gambling, it would be pretty much gone before he came home. So, whatever he had left over is what she had to use to buy the things we needed and to pay our bills. My mother was extremely good with money, very frugal. She knew how to make a dollar into ten dollars.

17

Though she had a rough marriage and life, in general, my mother was an upstanding woman. I don't know if she ever realized the woman, wife, and mother she really was, but looking back, my mom was a true Proverbs 31 woman.

"Who can find a virtuous wife? For her worth is far above rubies. The heart of her husband safely trusts her; So he will have no lack of gain. She does him good and not evil all the days of her life. She seeks wool and flax, And willingly works with her hands. She is like the merchant ships; She brings her food from afar. She also rises while it is yet night, And provides food for her household, And a portion for her maidservants. She considers a field and buys it; From her profits she plants a vineyard. She girds herself with strength, And strengthens her arms.

She perceives that her merchandise is good, And her lamp does not go out by night. She stretches out her hands to the distaff, And her hand holds the spindle. She extends her hand to the poor, Yes, she reaches out her hands to the needy. She is not afraid of snow for her household, For all her household is clothed with scarlet. She makes tapestry for herself; Her clothing is fine linen and purple.

Her husband is known in the gates when he sits among the elders of the land. She makes linen garments and sells them, And supplies sashes for the merchants. Strength and honor are her clothing; She shall rejoice in time to come. She opens her mouth with wisdom, And on her tongue is the law of kindness.

She watches over the ways of her household, And does not eat the bread of idleness. Her children rise up and call her blessed; Her husband also, and he praises her: "Many daughters have done well, But you excel them all." Charm is deceitful and beauty is passing, But a woman who fears the LORD, she shall be praised. Give her of the fruit of her hands, And let her own works praise her in the gates" Proverbs 31: 10-31, NKJV.

Abuse of any kind leaves individuals with deep seated trauma and torment in their lives. Their identities are stripped from them, and many never realize their full potential as human beings. Though my mother continued to be a wife, I am sure fulfilling all of her wifely duties, including being a full-time mother and homemaker, she was deeply broken as a woman. The strength and sheer perseverance of women in these abusive relationships and marriages is purely supernatural. I am sure that her faith in God had to be the single most reason that she stayed and endured so much pain and heartache.

Once again, I am not advocating for women to remain in abusive relationships; I am simply conveying the character of my mother and sharing her story with you. I wish she would have had the opportunity to experience a wonderful marriage and live a fulfilled life, but that was simply not her testimony. I know that what I witnessed my mother go through in her marriage directly affected me as a woman. I fully understand that what children see their parents endure, or go through, can and will serve as a blueprint of what their life may very well turn out to be.

Sadly, my childhood was laced with trauma and abuse from every side. From seeing the daily rage and alcoholism from my father, the horrific abuse my mother suffered, to the sexual abuse at the hand of my brother, there is no wonder I continued to suffer the things I encountered in my lifetime.

You may have experienced many similar things in your childhood. I pray that as I share transparently what I have gone through in my life that you will one, know that you are not alone, and two, that there is a light at the end of that dark tunnel. Hold on and if you hear anything in this message, may it be: NO MATTER HOW YOU FEEL, JESUS IS STILL ON THE THRONE! DON'T GIVE UP!

Chapter 2

Trauma Begins

"We are pressed on every side by troubles, but we are not crushed. We are perplexed, but not driven to despair. We are hunted down, but never abandoned by God. We get knocked down, but we are not destroyed—" 2 Corinthians 4:8-9, NLT.

When I was in the third grade, I used to berry pick in the summertime. I was a really competitive child, and they told us we would get fifty cents a crate, so I would calculate how much money I would make if I did a certain amount. I would hit that number every day. I think that has been a theme my entire life. I have always been very capable of solving issues, even though some were extremely hard. Unfortunately, I have gone through some tough situations in my life. I met a new girl in the third grade. She came to our school and she forgot her lunch. I asked the teacher if I could walk her home. She was a beautiful little girl. Her mother and father were divorced. She was a really sweet girl, and we became good friends. As we got to her home, I was trying to figure out what it was like to not have a mother and a father. I had both of my parents, but I came to find out, we had a lot of similar issues in our childhoods, so we connected well. I love her to this day.

I met my first boyfriend, Michael, in the 3rd grade. I would go to his house and play. He lived near me and his mom loved to sing and act, which were my favorite pastimes. I was in the play *Toyland* at six years old, a beautiful play about a child's dream. I was also taking piano lessons and I loved to sing. These were things that made me happy. Michael was nice and he really seemed to like me, so I decided I would like him, too. One day, he asked me if he could give me a ride home to my house. Michael weighed about 70lbs and I weighed 140lbs. I knew I couldn't ride on the back of his bike, but he insisted. Half way down Williams Street, Michael crashed the bike and he lost all his front teeth because of the crash. I felt so guilty like it was all my fault because I was a "fat cow". My mother always called me that name when she was mad at me. When we went to school the next day, the kids really made fun of me. Calling me *Bertha Butt* and *Bessie the Cow*. They all felt sorry for Michael and blamed me for the crash. I learned very early on that I couldn't do things other people could do because of my size and so I never tried again very often.

We cannot simply look at the outward appearance of people's lives and just assume they have it all together, or that they live happy lives. Some of the most lonely and depressed people have had both of their parents growing up, go to great schools, have all of the material things in life, and you would never know the trauma and torment that is going on behind closed doors. This is why it is so very important not to *judge a book by its cover*. Clearly, we live in a fallen world and we are all dealing with something. As humans, we judge by what we see on the outside, but God judges differently.

"The Lord doesn't see things the way you see them. People judge by outward appearance, but the Lord looks at the heart" 1 Samuel 16:7b, NLT.

My teacher in the third grade was an African American lady. My father was very racist and taught us racism at a very early age. Although I never agreed with it, I thought it was very ugly; I would say things that were racially motivated because that is how I was trained and taught. I remember one day, I said something that irritated her and she stomped on my feet. I do not remember exactly what I said, but I am sure I deserved it. Going into the fourth grade, I was really depressed. I was overweight and I did not feel pretty at all. I felt like kids were laughing at me all the time. I had an awkward face. It was really big and you could see the weight on my face. My hair was always important to me, but even then I did not like myself very much. I remember things in my home were getting extremely worse. There wasn't a lot of happiness in my life. I remember that food really was the center of my entire life in my childhood. Food was my only comfort. Food was what I went to for everything I was going through in my life.

"The poor will eat and be satisfied. All who seek the Lord will praise him. Their hearts will rejoice with everlasting joy" Psalm 22:26, NLT.

My appetite was not necessarily for natural food, it was longing for something, someone, that could fill the void in my life. Unfortunately, the more I ate, the harder it was for me to function. I did begin playing sports around the fourth and fifth grade. I played volleyball, basketball, and softball. It kept me active and connected with my friends, giving me something to do. Even then, I was still feeling very low in my life. I began to enter into puberty around eleven years old and this added to my depression. Going home was always hard for me. The daily witnessing my dad's alcohol addiction and his behavior, screaming and yelling, was really hard. I never learned that I could trust anyone. I was scared to death of everybody. I kept looking for that one person that I could trust. I kept looking for that place that would be safe. I remember as a little girl sleeping behind my mom and dad's door when my dad would finally fall asleep from his blackouts. I remember always feeling like there was a spirit of fear following me. I would feel like I was seeing ghosts, or something demonic, around in the dark and remembering how scary it was for me.

"For God has not given us a spirit of fear, but of power and of love and of a sound mind" 2 Timothy 1:7, NKJV.

When I saw the men in our backyard with my dad, walking in a circle, I thought they were devil worshippers; I wasn't really sure. For years, I thought it was some fake memory that I had but I found out from one of my siblings that my dad belonged to the Knights of Columbus, which is a demonic organization through the Catholic church. I believe that most of those men could have very well been from the Klan, I am not really sure. They were all Caucasian men and it was very demonic what they were doing out there in the dark.

The trauma at home became worse. One night, we came home and my dad had burned his car to the ground. We had to call 911 and the fire department showed up. My dad said he had burned it with a cigarette and they did not do anything about it. There were constant things like this happening in my childhood. I remember another time when I was in about the fourth grade and I woke up one Saturday morning with the sun beaming through the front door, which was wide open. Me and my little sister were the only ones home. My dad left us home while my mom was out with my twin sisters. It was very scary for us. I just remember feeling so alone, so desperately wanting someone to love me and to be my friend. I did feel like I had a lot of friends in school and talked to people on the phone, but I felt like I always had to buy them something for them to like me, or be my friend. I had to work for their love somehow, or listen to their problems and counsel them. I never felt like anyone was actually there for me.

"For God has said, "I will never fail you. I will never abandon you" Hebrews 13:5, NLT.

My understanding of Jesus, at this point, was not good. After the event that took place in my life at six years old when I walked up to a manger scene and it was not Jesus, I didn't know where He was in my life anymore. I did not know about the Holy Spirit. I was confirmed as a Catholic when I was twelve years old. They do have you go to classes so they can explain what the Catholic faith believes and what this means for you. All I remember feeling was that I was now a Catholic forever because I have three names. My aunt was a nun so I used her name as my third name. I used it as my confirmation name. It was all really just a joke as none of us knew what we were doing. I was getting further and further away from Jesus, needing the approval of others.

It is so very important for children to have a strong foundation of Christ in their family, for them to have a personal relationship with Him, even at a young age. They need to see Him at work in their family, through the good and bad times. No one is perfect, only Jesus, but we desperately need Him in our lives, in our marriages, and in our children's lives, so we can lean on Him when things are not always good. Learning and growing in Him is the greatest gift we could ever give to our children, so that when the storms of life hit, and they most certainly will, they know they can go to Him and find whatever they need.

My father became sober when I was about twelve or thirteen, around the fifth or sixth grade. The first week he went to treatment, I had my first blackout. Drugs and alcohol became the new way of life for me. I finally found something that was going to cover up the insecurity, the pain, the loneliness, and the lost soul. I was very broken and hurt. I just wanted to love someone, and for someone to love me. My mother was extremely sick due to my father's alcoholism. She was unable to nurture us the way she wanted to, but she did the best she could.

When I began moving into the six and seventh grades, kids were smoking cigarettes and marijuana. I don't think I was smoking marijuana that early, but I was smoking cigarettes because I wanted to be cool. I wanted to go to the girl/boy parties and to be accepted. It became an obsession for me to try to get people to like me, or love me. I made a very good friend in the seventh grade and we remained close throughout our high school years. I used to hang out with her all the time. There was a lot of sexual abuse in her family and her brother tried to sexually abuse me. I don't remember too much as I would close my eyes, but he was definitely coming on to me. I was so ashamed. He made fun of me and went around telling everyone what he had done, as if I had done something wrong. The entire time, I am just assuming this was another secret I was supposed to keep. There were always secrets in my family.

"For God will bring every work into judgment, Including every secret thing, Whether good or evil" Ecclesiastes 12:14, NKJV.

From the Green River to the Lily of the Valley

I hung out with my friend and we did drugs and drank alcohol together. She always had boyfriends because she was beautiful. I just wanted to be her friend because I loved her and she was sweet. Boys really did not like me in that way. They liked me as "friends," but I wasn't the *super-hot girl*. I was pretty but I was overweight. I just did not fit the criteria. My self-esteem got lower and lower. I just wanted to find a husband, so he could take me away from this horrible life I was living. I loved this girl and her family very much. I was always looking for families to love me, because I didn't feel love in my own family. She was also the most beautiful, strong girl I knew and I loved to follow her.

After my father became sober, he treated my mother like she was the Queen of England. They were very happy at that point. I did wonder sometimes though how happy they truly were due to his controlling spirit. He had a serious issue with control but at this point, she was able to get her sleep and rest unlike when he was addicted to alcohol. She began getting healthier and the dark circles under her eyes started to go away. They began to go to beaches all the time and on vacations. They were now living a much happier life than they had for many years. Unfortunately, I was now the one making her life hell because it was now me on drugs and drinking alcohol. It was now an everyday occurrence for me. Generational curses are real, and they must be dealt with in our lives quickly, so that our children will not repeat the same mistakes, errors, and addictions we have in our lives.

"Christ has redeemed us from the curse of the law, having become a curse for us (for it is written, "Cursed is everyone who hangs on a tree)" Galatians 3:13, NKJV.

As I began the eighth grade, I had my first boyfriend. His name was Tom. He promised me that he would love me. I was so excited! I had a boyfriend like all the other girls. I felt like I belonged and that I was important. He dumped me only after just a few weeks. He had given me a glow in the dark cross. Because I was so heartbroken, I walked into the class in front of everyone and threw it in his face. I found out what it felt like to be heartbroken… seriously heartbroken. My pride and my ego was shot. Kids were laughing at me and I was so embarrassed. I felt like a loser and that I was never going to have a boy that cared for me. It was horrible. It was painful. I really did not know what to do, so the drugs and the alcohol were my coping mechanism. Eating was still a problem, but now drugs and alcohol had taken the place of my addiction. My friends were now those that all did drugs and drank alcohol. I had grown up with most of these kids, and we had all come from alcoholic homes.

So now, I was the one who was holding and hiding secrets. I was the one steeped in drugs and alcohol. I was drinking in the park, going to parties, and meeting older boys that would take us places in their vans. I was putting myself in very dangerous situations. I was now doing horrific things. I was snorting cocaine, taking acid, drinking heavily, taking pills… whatever I could find that would make me high, and make me forget my reality. I was still a virgin, even though I had been molested as a child. I met a boy when I was sixteen, a neighbor. His name was Russell. He told me he loved me and that he would never leave me. He told me if I gave up my virginity to him that he would marry me. He got me this fake ring out of a candy machine, and I was just gullible enough and desperate enough to believe him. We had planned our big night and we were over my friend's house whose parents really did not monitor her very much. I remember I had the candles lit and it was going to be very romantic. I had a beautiful skirt on that my mom had made me. He was late getting there, and when he got there, he was drunk. His zipper was broken but it did not occur to me why or how the zipper would have broken. Later on, I found out that he had slept with another girl right before he came over to see me.

"Run from sexual sin! No other sin so clearly affects the body as this one does. For sexual immorality is a sin against your own body" 1 Corinthians 6:18, NLT.

I lost my virginity that night and I was devastated. He passed out drunk on me and did not say anything to me or comfort me. I was bleeding horrifically. I bled all over my skirt. I was nervous because my mom knew I was not on my period, so I had to get the skirt cleaned. I thought someone would find out I had lost my virginity simply by the look on my face. The fantasy of how wonderful making love to this man I thought I was going to marry turned into a nightmare. I continued to see him but I think he thought I was just someone he could have sex with because we lived by one another. When he got sick of it, he dumped me. The day he dumped me, I was devastated. I told him, "You promised me you would marry me. I gave you my virginity, which I assumed would only be for you, for marriage." It was really a big deal to me. I had listened to this in the Catholic church that you should wait until marriage and that it was really a God thing.

My friend's boyfriend lived in an area that was very rural up in the mountains, it was rustic and in the wooded area. We went to a party there one time, it was super fun but I felt really out of place. I got really drunk to deal with those feelings and passed out in a bedroom in the house, and I woke up to a boy with red hair raping me. I told him no and screamed but no one heard me because the music was too loud. All I remember is waking up with my stockings ripped and I was laying on the bathroom floor. I don't remember anything else and never told anyone out of fear that my friend wouldn't like me since that was her boyfriend's house. That was the 2nd of many rapes that would happen in my life from that point forward.

Though I had an upbringing in the Catholic church, there was no real living a life that was pleasing to God in our home. Abuse, alcoholism, sexual abuse, and dysfunction was our norm. But seemingly, in the back of my mind, I still *knew* what was right and what was wrong. Yet, I chose to do wrong and I suffered many consequences due to the dangerous decisions I made as a teenager. This would be just one of the many bad choices I would make throughout my life. We must surround ourselves with good people; not perfect, but those that desire to do good. Parents must be present in their children's lives, so that one, they know they are loved. Two, so that children are reared and guided along their journey of life, so that they are not swallowed up by the evil that seeks to destroy them. Unfortunately for me, my parents were simply not available for me, emotionally, mentally, or physically. Though they were getting their lives together, I had now spiraled out of control.

Russell and I were walking home and he got very angry. He was drinking and had a beer bottle. He stopped and broke the bottle and was going to slit my throat because I would not stop following him and begging him to stay with me. This was near my father's house. He was still in AA (Alcoholics Anonymous) at this time. He saw us out of the window and shut the curtains because he did not want to see my drama. The neighbors had to call 911 because I was literally about to be killed. I was on my hands and knees begging him not to leave me. That is how desperate I was at this point. For the next nine months, I was severely depressed. I moved in with a young lady that lived down near the park by our house. She was not a Catholic school kid, she went to public school. Her parents let her smoke pot at home, so it was a perfect location for me.

I eventually went to St. Mary's Catholic Academy, a girl's only school, my freshman and sophomore year. There were a lot of rich girls that went there. I was made fun of a lot and called many names for being overweight. I was always told I had a pretty smile, but that I needed to lose weight. I knew how to mask the hurt, pain, and disappointment by simply smiling. I had gone through so much trauma in my childhood that I was broken, and broken beyond comprehension in my eyes, at that time. I did have a belief in Jesus, but I was very sad and broken. I eventually went to high school and got a job working at a nursing home after school feeding elderly people. Life was really hard at this point. I had to go to school, do homework, and then go to work. I began to drink more and go to parties, hanging out with old friends again. I finally got to the point that I no longer wanted to be at St. Mary's Academy and after my sophomore year, I begged my father to send me to Jefferson High School. He was so livid! He picked up a chair in the dining room and threw it up against the wall. He was so mad at me. But I needed to know what it was like to be around other kids and most importantly, I could drink and do drugs at Jefferson. So, Jefferson won.

"And "don't sin by letting anger control you." Don't let the sun go down while you are still angry" Ephesians 4:26, NLT.

I began to date a man much older than me, he was twenty-five and I was sixteen and a half. He had a lot of marijuana, so me and my friend would smoke all the time and began to steal, do stronger drugs, and just living a fast life. I stopped going to school. Suicide was on my mind all the time, but strangely enough, I was chicken. I was too scared to take my life, so the devil could not mess with me in this particular area. The spirit of fear kept me from killing myself. How ironic, huh? We were sitting at a park one night and I remember looking at the bottom of the bottle I was drinking. I thought to myself, this is not working anymore. I am not getting high like I used to, it's not fun, it's not taking the pain away, and I was looking for what was next. One day, I was drinking heavily, taking cocaine, smoking marijuana, and I was with a boy my age and we took some LSD. I very well could have overdosed this night. I was seeing blue spots, having hallucinations, and began seeing snakes. I was engulfed in demonic activity.

I was very sick emotionally, spiritually, and mentally at this point. I got really drunk one night at John's house. John was kind and very handsome, and I wished he would like me but he used to date one of my best friends, so he was hands off. Instead, I tried to commit suicide for attention by taking his mother's pills in the bathroom. John sat up with me all night talking. My addiction had completely taken over in my life, I was slowly but surely dying from alcohol and drug addiction. Another time, I was at a party that John was at, I was flirting with him and begged him to walk me home. When we got to my house, we were kissing and I let him sneak into my parents' house with me. Up the stairs we went falling down drunk and we started having sex in my sister's bed which broke, so we moved to my room. I was terrified my mom would catch us but I was too drunk to really care. I became pregnant this night.

If I am to be honest, I manipulated him into this. I needed someone like him to want me, I was desperately sick and lonely; now a baby, what was I going to do? I knew this baby would not be healthy with all of the alcohol I was drinking and the drugs I was doing. I knew my parents were going to be extremely angry with me, and potentially throw me out of the house. I was terrified, but I made the decision to get an abortion. It was the most horrible day of my entire life. I remember getting there and the protestors were outside shaming me and throwing things at me. I had this robe with a hood on it and felt so low walking into the clinic. I can still remember the things they were saying to me about the baby. He was a boy. He would have been my only "white" baby, as I later married an African American man and had biracial children. He probably would have been a blond haired, blue-eyed baby boy. I was almost twenty weeks, so he was a pretty good sized baby when he came out.

I was so depressed that they had to give me valium, and a lot of it. I drank and got drunk that night, and every night for the next year. This was in November and by April, I was really high on acid, cocaine, and LSD. The boy I was with had been getting high all day. He lived in a house with his windows boarded up all the time. We were walking and I was so high. I did not know where I was, so I asked him to take me home. He walked me home and my mother woke up and then proceeded to wake up my father. I remember the look on her face; she must have known I was high. My dad, a recovering alcoholic, walking through his own 12-step program, was now trying to walk his daughter through the principles. I sat in the living room, walls like they were breathing, and I was hallucinating. I got up and went into the bathroom. It was there that God met me and said to me, "Do you really want to continue living like this? Because you are going to die like this." I told Him that I did not want to die like this.

"These desires give birth to sinful actions. And when sin is allowed to grow, it gives birth to death" James 1:15, NLT.

I came out and told my father everything I had been doing from the alcohol to the drugs and how long I had been doing it, and that I wanted help. Finally, I went to bed around 4 o'clock in the morning. When I woke up, I was like, "Oh my God! I just confessed to everything. I am going to have to change, or they are going to put me out of here." They took me to an AA meeting the next day, and things began to change, or so I thought.

It was at this point in my life where, even though my father was an addict and my mother was his punching bag, full of faults themselves, I was finally beginning to see that they were doing their very best to help me, and that they did not want me to go through what they had gone through. They listened to me confess all that I had done, and there was no judgment. The Bible says that *we all sin and fall short of the glory of God*. I love those two people so very much and have forgiven them both. I am so glad that I know they are both with Jesus in Heaven. My greatest healing in my life was forgiving my parents.

"But when you are praying, first forgive anyone you are holding a grudge against, so that your Father in heaven will forgive your sins, too" Mark 11:25, NLT.

At my first AA meeting, I met a man named Kenny White. He had his head down on the table, not listening to anything anyone had to say. When I walked in, he peeked his head up and looked at me. It was not normal for a seventeen year old girl to be in Alcoholics Anonymous in 1980. God was about to save my life. And He was saving my life through all of the trauma, turmoil, and tragedies I had gone through in my childhood. I could see that His hand was always with me, making sure I was safe. He had a greater purpose for my life. I did not see it then, but I absolutely can see it now. I went to ninety meetings in ninety days and did all they asked me to do. I got a sponsor and changed my playground; I let go of all the old people in my life that I hung out with and started to make new friends.

One new friend's name was Rosemary. We've been friends now for about forty-two years. I love her to this day. I prayed for a friend, and God brought me Rosemary. We had so much fun together in our recovery. We would go to the hot springs and lay out in the sun, go out for pizza, and we had to learn how to have fun without the need for alcohol and drugs. It was very foreign, but it was fun. I was beginning to find out what joy was really like. I got a great job at a hospital making good money for my age. I bought a car and got my driver's license. I began to get healthy and trying to lose weight. I started to go dancing at the discotech for underage kids. That was a fun hobby, but then I began to feel the loneliness once again. I began to feel empty again. I did not know what was causing this to creep up again in my life. At AA, they taught me about God, but I really did not understand who He was, and what He was doing in my life.

I began to go to a disco tech underage in Beaverton, Oregon. It was called "EarthQuake Ethels". I would save all my money to buy new outfits to go to the club. I was a great dancer but yet no boys seemed to like me. I so desperately wanted and needed a boy to want me to fill the empty hole that drugs and alcohol and food used to fill. I would meet random men and sleep with some, not all, but no one seemed interested in being in a relationship and for me, the sex was simply a tool to find a husband. As backward as that sounds, I was intensely lonely.

The God I had been raised up with, I did not believe He wanted me because of all I had done. I did not believe He would forgive me. The abortion (murder), losing my virginity before marriage, and being raped… these were all major sins to me, and I just simply could not wrap

35

my mind around a holy God forgiving such an unholy person. I just did not know Him, the real Him. I certainly was not going to live at my parents' house and leave the Catholic religion. My dad would have had a heart attack, so I really did not know what to do at that time. I really did not even want to get to know who He was, but what I had missed out on in AA is that God is the entire foundation of your recovery. I began to revert back to my old lifestyle by sleeping around with men and trying to fill that empty hole in my life. Life just began to become boring to me. I eventually ran into an old friend from high school that had been a go-go dancer, and a prostitute. We went up to the Rose Gardens in Portland one night and we sat there looking over the beautiful lights of the city and she began to tell me about this glamorous life she had been living. What she was actually doing was trying to groom me for her pimp. Pimps teach their prostitutes to groom other women to bring them into the fold to make more money for that man. I had no idea, at first, that this is what she was doing, but I eventually learned the hard way.

"Meanwhile, my enemies lay traps to kill me. Those who wish me harm make plans to ruin me. All day long they plan their treachery" Psalm 38:12, NLT.

Chapter 3

Groomed & Trafficked

"The thief does not come except to steal, and to kill, and to destroy. I have come that they may have life, and that they may have it more abundantly." John 10:10, NKJV

I had a spirit of fear, anxiety, and torment that traveled with me all of my life until my late fifties due to all of the childhood trauma that I experienced. I could not function properly. I was scared of everything. I would not go roller-skating and do other activities because of my weight. As I got older, it became a lot harder.

"Do not be deceived: "Evil company corrupts good habits."
1 Corinthians 15:33

We cannot expect to experience real change, or even transformation, in our lives if we are not adamant about changing the people we hang around and the circles we frequent. Not one person on this Earth is above temptation and this is why it is so very important to guard ourselves, and our children, from things that are sure to destroy us, and them. It doesn't matter how *good* of a Christian you are, or how good of a person you purpose to be; sin is waiting at the door for all of us. God's Word was given to us to be a safeguard for our lives. I just truly wish I would have had the opportunity at a young age to have it covering my life and my home.

We are born into a fallen world, and I was really being attacked by the devil and didn't even realize I was being attacked. I remained in this state for several more years as I was continuing to drink heavily. I went to parties and would get many people mad at me because I would talk too much or simply did things just to irritate people because I was filthy drunk. There was not a day in my teenage years that I was not drunk or high. No boys liked me and I had very few friends.

"I can never escape from your Spirit!
I can never get away from your presence!
If I go up to heaven, you are there;
if I go down to the grave, you are there.
If I ride the wings of the morning,
if I dwell by the farthest oceans,
even there your hand will guide me,
and your strength will support me.
I could ask the darkness to hide me
and the light around me to become night—
but even in darkness I cannot hide from you.
To you the night shines as bright as day.
Darkness and light are the same to you." Psalm 139:7-12, NLT

The proposition by my go-go dancer friend, I entertained. I thought to myself that this would be fun. I was bored and she said all I had to do was dance. It wasn't that big of a deal. She told me that I did not have to take my clothes off and that I could just wear sexy costumes. I thought sure, I can do this. She told me that I would be making good tips, and I got really excited about this. She then introduced me to her pimp. Of course, she did not tell me he was her pimp but that he used to be her boyfriend. I started seeing him and boy did he groom me quickly! He took me to fancy hotels and we became sexually involved. I thought that was what love was all about at that point. I equated sex with love because that is all that men wanted from me. Going back even to my childhood and my father, I was deathly afraid to tell him my feelings because of fear of rejection, abandonment, and him simply not understanding. I carried these fears into all of my relationships, or situations, with other men.

So, this guy Derrick, the pimp, began to convince me that I needed to move to Seattle with him and start this new life. He told me that he loved me and that he would never leave me. He told me that we could get a house and be together forever, and that I could dance because I was such a good dancer. I fell in love with him right away, just as I did with every guy I met, because I did not know what true love meant.

"We love Him because He first loved us" 1 John 4:19, NKJV.

Again, I did not have a healthy view of love in my life. My childhood experiences of seeing my father abuse my mother, being sexually abused and assaulted, and even being molested by my own brother left deep seated wounds that were never healed. In this, it was just a matter of time before I would spiral down another dark path in my life looking for and seeking either someone to love me, or somewhere to feel accepted. If we do not know who we are and how very valuable and precious we are to God, we can and will accept any sort of substitute.

When we compromise and sell ourselves short of self-worth, we are not receiving God's best for our lives.

Obviously, it wasn't true love because God was not anywhere in the picture. I eventually left with this gentleman, making my parents very angry. Mind you, Derrick was black and my father was a huge racist. He told me if I left with this black man that I could never come back home. He pretty much shut the door on me. I left with Derrick and moved to Seattle. The first week I was there, I wrecked my car, which left me completely dependent upon him. They didn't have cell phones in 1980. The guy that I hit was a nightclub owner and he was the first person I ever turned a trick with, as a prostitute. When I got there, Derrick did not have a house for me. He put me in a motel. He didn't live with me, but with another woman, which I did not know about, and I did have to take my clothes off in the go-go joint. The first time he took me to work, I told him I could not work because I was on my period. He choked me until I saw white stars in my eyes, or white spots. He told me that I would go to work and do what he says. I knew at that point that I had made a huge mistake.

So, I began my career as a go-go dancer and a prostitute. This was not originally what I thought I would be doing, but here I was making a lot of money. Unfortunately, he would not let me keep the money. I had to give it all to him. He did not sleep at my motel with me, so I was always alone. He had his best friend and another prostitute living next door to watch me. He must have gotten a kickback for watching me. The neighbor actually had a transvestite brother who I actually liked as a person. He was okay, but I was completely scared of the entire group of them. I was still clean and sober at this time and trying to stay that way, but life was deteriorating very quickly. I started turning tricks after working 12-14 hour shifts dancing every single day of the week. Sometimes, I would get Sundays off but typically, I still had to work. Derrick was very violent if I did not do exactly what he told me to do. He would beat me, and then he brought his pit bull to my hotel room because he knew I was scared of them. He would leave the dog at the end of my bed so I wouldn't leave, as I had threatened to do so. The dog would bark at me if I even moved, so I would pee in the bed because Derrick was gone, and I could not get out of the bed, sometimes for 12-14 hours.

He would not give me money for food, so I would scrounge up coins from my tricks, so I could go down the street for breakfast and have an omelet in the morning. I was losing weight which was good because I was overweight, but it was definitely not the way I wanted to lose it. The owners of the club I worked at were of the mafia. One of the ladies would snatch my money out of my hand and give it to Derrick. They all worked together. The club was being watched but I really didn't understand all that was going on. I knew it was illegal, the prostitution and all of that, but I really did not understand all of the ins and outs of the mafia and what they did.

I started to become paranoid because I thought everyone was out to get me. It was truly demonic, probably the most demonic period in all my life. No one in my circle could I trust, not one! At least when I was home, I could somewhat trust my parents, in my mind. I could definitely trust my sisters but my family was backing off from me, which was understandable. I had a few people I could trust in Portland, but in Seattle, I could trust no one. With the paranoia setting in, I relapsed and began to drink. One day, I went over to visit the pimp that was living next door and they were smoking crack. I was turned on to crack and boy oh boy, I hit that pipe and never put it down. I told Derrick, my pimp, if he ever let me get loaded, I would be useless to him. I told him I was an alcoholic and an addict, first and foremost, but he didn't listen to me.

After the first year of prostituting for him, I began to deteriorate. The club was being watched by the police because it was a very well-known mob family that owned it. I had no idea I was turning tricks with police officers and vice officers and I had a very big mouth, at times. I was giving them all of the information about the club, not realizing what I was doing, or that they were the police. They ended up closing the club and I did not have a job. I was now useless to this pimp that had brought me to Seattle. My father would have nothing to do with me at that point. I used to call from closets crying and asking him to please help me. I would tell him that Derrick was beating me that day and that I had nowhere to go and no money. I begged him to help me and to please let me come home. My dad would have nothing to do with me. I would call my friend Marcy and cry, asking her to help me, but she was my age. How was she going to help me?

I was eighteen at this time. It was a horrible couple of years being trafficked and imprisoned. There was so much sadness and turning these tricks were so gross and nasty. The smell of the men was horrific and the things they would say to me and the things they wanted me to do were sickening. I would not even get the benefit of the money because it was being taken from me. I was being used over and over again. All I came there for was love. I was desperately looking for love in all the wrong places. The drug use got extremely bad. I began smoking crack with a propane tank. One time, I had been smoking crack for about three days and fell asleep on the bed in the motel with the propane still going. I am lucky I am alive. Nothing but God again watching over me.

From the Green River to the Lily of the Valley

"For He Himself has said, "I will never leave you nor forsake you" Hebrews 13:5b, NKJV.

Though I made some very dangerous and destructive choices in my life, I always had this strange feeling like God was with me, watching over me. Though I was ashamed and felt unworthy of His love and forgiveness, He was still, somehow, lingering in my thoughts, and at times, in my prayers. Many of us choose to live any kind of way we want, but when the consequences of those choices catch up with us, we tend to cry out to Him to help us, to save us from our bad decisions. God is full of grace and mercy, and yes, He loves us so very much and will forgive us if we repent and turn away from our sin. But if we continue in our sin, not heeding His voice of correction and warning, we are left to suffer the consequences of our choices. May we learn to hear His voice quickly and obey, so that we do not find ourselves in dangerous and destructive positions.

Eventually, Derrick left me and had not paid for my motel room. They were getting ready to throw me out into the street. I was too drunk and too high to figure out how to survive without the nightclub. I did not know how to be a street girl because I was not a street prostitute at that point. I found a treatment program to come and get me called the *Conquest Center*. They came and picked me up and brought me to their program where I remained in detox for the next three days.

My life had spiraled out of control.

Chapter 4

The Green River Killer

"He who dwells in the secret place of the Most High shall abide under the shadow of the Almighty. I will say of the Lord, "He is my refuge and my fortress; My God, in Him I will trust." Psalm 91:1-2, NKJV

I had come out of the detox program and they had allowed all the girls in the program to steal my clothes and what little money I had left, and all of my cologne. So, I had nothing left. Basically, all my nice stuff was stolen. I got really angry and they put me on the hot seat in front of the entire group in the program. I was probably one of only three Caucasian women in the entire group. They pretty much began to taunt me and tell me that I love to give my money to black men. This was certainly not therapeutic for me, but very racist. It was horrible. Keep in mind, I came from a home with a very racist father and I grew up in a predominantly African American neighborhood. I was taught confusion about race from as early on as I can remember. The one thing I hated the most was the hatred that my father spewed out of his mouth about other cultures. One thing I was trying to get across to them was that I did not feel this way, as my father did, and that me choosing

Derrick and going into environments that my father would never approve of was proof of me not being racist.

"There is no longer Jew or Gentile, slave or free, male and female. For you are all one in Christ Jesus" Galatians 3:28, NLT.

My heart was in the right place about people of other ethnicities, so this really angered me. They were trying to help me get clean and sober, but I took it the wrong way. I tried to find a way to get away from there because they took everything I owned. There was a guy that lived next door to the home. I would wave at him and I finally snuck outside to meet him. I befriended him only for the purpose of getting me out of there. One day we left, but I could not get any of my belongings that they had taken from me, so one of my tricks, Richard, that I had met at the go-go club, got me a motel room for thirty days. He was going to help me go to college and get clean and sober, but once I got to the motel, everything came rushing back. I could not stay sober.

I moved into the ACE Motel on 88th and Aurora Ave N., Seattle, WA. I met a sweet girl named Sandra Majors. She was my age, and a prostitute trying to leave her pimp. We both were going to help each other go to college and do better. Sandra was from Rochester, NY. We would go work the streets together just to pay our motel fee and then we would laugh and talk and dream together. She was becoming my very best friend. She couldn't read or write, so I wrote a letter for her to send to her mother about how good she was doing. I loved helping people. It was the one thing that made me feel good. One day, we went to the corner store at 90th and Aurora. There was a small laundromat in the back and they sold teriyaki. We got some lunch and went and sat on the dryers to keep warm. A camper pulled up to the door and was trying to solicit Sandra and me.

First, the man in the camper really wanted me to go with him, he promised me $300 for the day, which was way more than anyone would ever offer us on the streets in 1982. The guy had on police pants, a V-neck t-shirt, and socks with no shoes. Also, he was in a camper in the back of the camper. I just wasn't comfortable. Everything inside me said NO, don't go with this guy. So, Sandra said, "I will go with him;" I begged her not to go. Something just didn't seem right here. Call it intuition, I believe Jesus stopped me that day and He was trying to stop Sandra, too, but she didn't listen to the warning. Three hours went by and she didn't return. I woke up the next day, still no Sandra and all she owned was in her room, so I knew she would come back. I thought maybe she went back to her pimp, but still she wouldn't have left all she owned. I had seen T.V. news reports about a man in a camper killing women. I didn't have a good feeling. I knew something really wrong must have happened.

Christmas Eve of 1982, I called the King County Police Department and reported Sandra as missing. I had seen her real ID from NY with her real name, Sandra Majors. I told this to the person who took my information, they transferred me to the Green River Task Force, and I shared all my information with them. Now, I wait to see what happens. Sandra was my only lifeline at that point, my only real friend in the whole world and now she was gone... what do I do now? I would spend the next thirty-four years wondering how to name and bury this sweet woman...

I started to go to nightclubs at night. I started to get a little freedom because I did not have a pimp like before. I began to teach myself how to turn tricks on the street to get money. I was scared to death, but I learned how to do it. I wasn't very good at it, as I stayed in jail all the time. One night, I went to a nightclub and I met a man named Charles, pimp number two. He wasn't a sworn pimp; he was more of what they called a *hustler*. He had a criminal background that I did not know about, at that time, that was very serious. I was not good at picking men, as I stated earlier. I just seemed to attract men that had crimes against women. We got high and he told me a story about him going to prison, and I was going to fix him and take care of him just like I was when I first met Derrick. He would tell me about his Korean mother and his African American father and all about the Korean War, and this is what led him to become a pimp. I felt so sorry for him and believed him.

Both of these men used me and manipulated me for their own gain. People that are bleeding, will bleed on you. They may have some good intentions to do good but they are bleeding so fast themselves that they are bound to bleed on you, as well. I began to see Charles and he was a little different in that I figured him to be a long-term relationship guy, as he introduced me to his mom. Unfortunately, I sat on her porch and she told him that she was not letting that "white girl" in her house. I began to cry and cry, pleading with her to let me in because I did not have anywhere to go. Again, my dad was not letting me back in his house. I begged my mom to let me come back home, but in some way, I was angry with myself for letting this man manipulate me and take all my money. Charles' stepdad, Daddy Earl, told Alice, Charles' mom, to *let that white girl in the house.* So, I came into her home and Alice made me sit on a towel like I was nasty or dirty. I did it just to keep the peace. As the years went on, Alice and I became the very best of friends. It's amazing what can happen if you just allow a person a little room to vent their hurts, how they will come around.

I went back to living the motel life and began to turn tricks the best way I knew how to survive. I had a trick named Richard who was a mechanical engineer for a local college. He was well renowned in his field. He never had sex with me, he was a good man. I don't know what I brought for him, maybe some fantasy, but he never hurt me in any way. He tried to help me as much as he could. I began to see Charles again and we were getting closer and closer. He introduced me to a buddy friend of his that was in prison whose wife was a prostitute. They were going to teach me the ropes. What Charles didn't know was that they were conspiring to steal me from him because that is what that life was all about. She took me to a party and I got extremely drunk and began to steal men's money from them, taking their coats and shoving them down laundry vents. I blacked out and they took me to their house and they raped me at gunpoint. They both raped me and it was frightening and nauseating. Thinking about it to this day makes me very sick. I have worked greatly on forgiveness and have forgiven them, but the memory is still very horrible for me.

When I woke up the next morning, they were sleeping in the living room and I was in their bed. They had intended on keeping me for their own use. I was not having it. I found five hundred dollars rolled up in a rubber band, which was her bail money. It used to cost five hundred dollars to be bailed out for prostitution. So, I took the money, a fur coat, and I found a diamond ring, and was going to sell it all. I got out of there and made it to Fred Meyers in Kent. My motel was all the way up North but I was too hungover to take a bus that far. I met a girl that worked at

Fred Meyers and told her all that had happened. She told me she would take me home after work.

By the time I got to the Ace Motel on 88th and North Aurora in Seattle, the two that had raped me were in my motel with a gun. The owner of the motel must have let them in because they paid him. I had to eat humble pie at this moment because of what I did. They took me back to their apartment and raped me again. They raped me a few times for the next four or five days. I was terrified and did not know what to do. I was truly being held hostage. They would not let me talk to Charles. He was scared and did not know where they lived. They sent me to a massage parlor, of which I had never worked before, in Bremerton, Washington where the Army boys are stationed. I had to live there and work there for twenty four hours a day for two weeks from the 1st to the 15th, as these were their paydays. I made a lot of money but of course, the house mother kept the money. She did give me half back, though I do not believe she really gave me half. I believe I had made around $3000.00 in those two weeks.

"For the love of money is the root of all kinds of evil. And some people, craving money, have wandered from the true faith and pierced themselves with many sorrows" 1 Timothy 6:10, NLT.

I was supposed to go back to Charles' so-called friend's house (the married pimp couple) who had all of my childhood clothing and memorabilia. Childhood pictures that I had saved and albums like Earth, Wind & Fire who I loved so much. Everything that connected me to my childhood, to Susie Brady as a child. I decided to go back to Seattle and call the Vice Squad to help free me of this life. Now, this was against everything that I believed because I did not trust the police at all. But I called them and told them everything that was going on and that I was being held hostage. I told them that I needed help out because I was afraid that they would kill me. Even though my parents did not want me, I was going to go home to Portland and find a way to live. They knew who he was because he was a violent offender. He had murdered someone in the past and went to prison. He had always been a pimp and prostituting women was his way of life. They wanted me to go meet him and give him money, so they could arrest him for promoting prostitution. They promised me that they would take me to their apartment to get my things and then put me on a bus to Portland where I would be safe.

I trusted them. I was staying at the Edgewater Inn. I have always had champagne taste on a beer budget. It is a very expensive motel in Downtown Seattle. I was drinking my way to success again, looking for *Mr. Richy Rich* to do whatever, and waiting on the police to help me. I went to the event and gave him the money. They arrested him for promoting prostitution. He swiftly told me he was going to kill me. He did not stay in jail long, he was out within a month or two. Apparently, the charge did not stand. The police said, "Sorry, we cannot get your things because we need a search warrant to get into his house." They also told me that they don't give bus tickets to help people get home. So, I had just put myself in a very dangerous position being a snitch and had no way out. I went back to the Edgewater where I was staying. It was very expensive and the $3000.00 I got from the massage parlor was quickly gone. I called Charles and he immediately came and got me. He let me move in with his mother at that point. We began working the streets and got a place in the U District. We got our own apartment.

I was still drinking and doing drugs off and on. Charles was now trying to recruit young girls to pimp out. He was always looking for underage girls to get more money for us. Again, he was not really a pimp but a hustler. He knew how to dress up and go to the bars and talk to rich, wealthy men telling them how to invest in businesses that were never going to happen. They would write him checks and then cancel them later. He was bisexual, so I do believe there were sexual things going on. He was a very dangerous man, too. I was just trying to figure out what I was going to do. I would walk the streets of Downtown Seattle from 10pm-2am selling my body while Charles would sit at a local restaurant. I was raped again, robbed, beaten… I should have been dead many times over. Not to mention, I went to jail multiple times.

One time, I was with a girl named Kelly McGinnis. I had met her Downtown and we went to jail because we had turned a trick with two guys we later found out were policemen. We went to the motel, and Richard Guise was the Vice Cop that arrested me. He was a sweet, big teddy bear of a police officer. If you are reading this book Richard Guise, I love you. You were a lifesaver for me that day. Here I was barely eighteen years old and being arrested for the first time. I literally peed my pants, I was so scared.

He was so kind and treated me well. He didn't do what the other Vice Cops did to us afterwards. He took me and Kelly to jail and it was the weekend, of course, which means we didn't get to see the judge until Monday. Kelly held my hand all the way in the jail. I was so freaking scared as I had never been to jail before. I was terrified. We were in a dormitory style jail cell where everyone could see you going to the bathroom. It was just a very open environment. She hung out with me the entire weekend which I am so grateful to her for. I went back in a few weeks later because I was not very good at working the streets. When I went back in, the matron said to me, "You know the girl that you were with the last time you were here?" I said, "Yes," and she said, "She was killed by the Green River Killer." I began to cry. She was the fourth victim of serial killer Gary Ridgway, the Green River Killer. He was one of the greatest fears for us women working the streets in Seattle and around Washington state in the 1980s and 90s. He was active, alive and well, and killing women all over the state. They said he only killed 49 women, but I believe it was many more.

Months later, the Green River Task Force called to let me know they may have found Sandra Majors' body and reached out to me and let me know. They could not find her name anywhere in the system. They stated that she had never been arrested there, at least not under the name of Sandra Majors. She also did not have any dental records, so they could not trace her that way, either. King County reached out to me for years asking if I had any more information. I told them that I saw her ID card and the name clearly said: *Sandra Majors*. I asked them why they could not simply reach out to her family. For thirty-four years, she was an unnamed and unclaimed victim of the Green River Killer. It wouldn't be until many years later that the world would meet Sandra Majors. I will spend my entire life keeping her name alive. She mattered, she was a person who was a sister, a daughter, a friend. Keep reading to watch the Glory of God in this story…

"Those who want to get rich fall into temptation and a trap and into many foolish and harmful desires that plunge people into ruin and destruction" 1 Timothy 6:9, NKJV.

Chapter 5

"Have mercy on me, O Lord, for I am weak; O Lord, heal me, for my bones are troubled." Psalm 6:2, NKJV

On June 1, 1982, I had enough of drinking and doing drugs. I went back to my first AA meeting again and got a job in a nursing home. I worked really hard to get sober and clean. Charles asked his mother if I could move in again with her in the Central District of Seattle, and a month later, I found out I was pregnant. This was my first child, Elliot. Although I was terrified, I was excited because I loved Charles. He may not have been the perfect man given the fact that he was very violent and a drug addict, but I felt comfortable and stable living with his family. Charles' sister was a heroin addict and hated white women, so she was very awful towards me. Charles' mom also did not like white women, but his father was very nice to me. I found out that she had been a slave, so I understood her hatred towards white people. I felt I was obligated to extend mercy to them based upon what she had gone through. Though it was not perfect, I lived this way for many years.

My life was always one roller coaster after another; I never really felt like I had a time of peace and happiness. I was constantly in some kind of confusion whether it was of my own doing, or from those that I was surrounded with on a daily basis. I found myself always wanting to just please people to keep the peace. I was not living, I was simply surviving. So many people living on the streets are walking through life numb and out of touch with reality. Decision making is not based off of wisdom, but desperation. Throughout this book, I truly want you to try to understand the deep-rooted pain and trauma that many of us that lived in the streets suffered. The wounds are real, and many never find healing and deliverance in their lives. There is a heaviness and darkness that is incomprehensible. There is no rest. Remember, you can pick your sin, but you cannot pick your consequences.

"So what do people get in this life for all their hard work and anxiety? Their days of labor are filled with pain and grief; even at night their minds cannot rest. It is all meaningless" Ecclesiastes 2:22-23, NLT.

One day, on my way home from work at the nursing home, I saw a man shot and killed on Martin Luther King Way. His name was Blue and he was a doorman at a place called Dino's. I loved Dino's, it was a fun place to go and have fun, but the environment I was in was very scary. It was similar to where I grew up in the Central District of Portland with low income issues and drug addiction. It was just a lot going on being that I was pregnant trying to figure out how I was going to raise a child. I had made up in my mind that I was absolutely not having another abortion at this point. I was going to have this child and find a way to deal with it.

56

One night, I was upstairs as Charles was not home. He was always gone at night and never came home. When he did come home, he was always drunk and high and I knew he had been having sex with other women. He was very violent so I did not want to bring it up and get beat by him. I wanted to protect my baby, so I stayed silent. I would hide in the room hoping his sister would not come in the room shooting at me. His mother would shoot a gun up the stairs at his sister when they would get mad at one another. It was a very toxic and violent environment I was living in. I was looking under his bed and found court papers. He told me he had gone to prison for drug issues but as I am looking up at the top of the court papers, it states that he is listed as a Class A Psychopath.

I began to read more about him and he had been convicted of raping many women. He was a serial rapist in the Seattle area at one time. I am sitting there in shock thinking I am about to have a baby by this man who is a serial rapist. I questioned what my son was going to be like. I didn't understand all of this but I was asking myself what I had done and how this would be psychologically for my unborn son. I believed I was in grave danger. I didn't know what to do or where to go. I had nowhere to turn and no one that cared.

When I met Charles, he told me horrific stories about his childhood. His mother, who had been a slave owner's child, was not biracial but she was her biological parents' child. Most of her sisters were products of the slave owner and rape and were biracial due to rape of her mother on the plantation. His mother hated Caucasian people, and possibly and rightfully so, at that point in her life. She was very broken and violent, and also an alcoholic. Although she had married a wonderful man, all men to her were tricks. She was very good at manipulating people out of money. He would tell me horrific stories of her tying him underneath of a bed, while she would turn a trick with a customer when he was a little boy. She instilled violent anger within him at a very early age against white people, especially against white women. Horrible anger and hatred. So, I believe this was his reasoning for raping white women, mostly in empty buildings.

Here I am with a seriously dangerous man. How could I tell my family? I did eventually tell my mom and she said she would work on my dad, but he was not having it. He was not going to let me come home. I was eighteen years old and pregnant, turning nineteen. My stay at the nursing home did not last very long. I was still turning tricks off and on to make money once in a while. I was trying to abstain from it being I was pregnant. I had been to jail so many times. They had this thing called SOAP: Stay Out of Areas of Prostitution. I was always going back to jail on probation violations because I would not stay out of these areas. I was a hardheaded teenager. I wanted to go shopping at Nordstroms which was in this area.

One Christmas Eve, Charles and I had a big fight. I was pregnant with my son and we had no money. His mother was throwing us out of the house, so I needed to go and make some money. I went downtown and it was snowing. I had high heels on with no stockings, a short skirt, and no coat while pregnant. I was on 2nd and Pike and just alone. I don't even know how to explain how alone I felt. It was Christmas Eve with no family and even with my baby in my belly, I was the loneliest I had ever been in my life. I met this man and he was staying at the hotel on the corner. He gave me a big whopping forty bucks, and he wanted to do horrible things to me. I was so desperate for money that I let him do whatever he wanted to me. It was the most horrible and devastating thing that has ever happened to me on the streets. I was at my lowest. It was Christmas and though I knew of Jesus, I had pretty much given up on Him at this point in my life.

How could He let all of these things happen to me? Why did He not stop the abuse? The molestation? The rapes? The beatings? These are not merely my own questions throughout my life; many men and women in the streets have asked these very same questions over and over again, not understanding how a loving God could just sit back and let these things happen to people. Well, most of us did not know about free will, or the choice to choose to rise above the things that may have happened in our childhoods. Most do not understand that we live in a sinful world and evil and wicked things happen around us every day, to all people. Some situations are out of our control, especially as children, but eventually, as we become adults, we do know right from wrong. Unfortunately, so many in the streets have fallen so deep into the pits of hell on Earth that they don't know how to find their way back to a normal life. There is nothing wrong with God. He is always waiting patiently with arms outstretched, ready and willing to welcome us home as we desperately seek Him with our whole hearts. His love is everlasting toward us.

"Long ago the Lord said to Israel: "I have loved you, my people, with an everlasting love. With unfailing love I have drawn you to myself" Jeremiah 31:3, NLT.

But here is honestly one of the greatest problems for those either living in the streets, dealing in prostitution, drug dealing, drug and alcohol addictions, and sexual addictions, or even those living in million dollar homes wanting for nothing financially… they do not know, and have not experienced, authentic love. Not from their father, their mother, their siblings, extended family members, and most importantly, God. We are internally wired, no matter if we say we believe in God or not, to equate the love, or lack thereof, from those that birthed us to our Creator. Many people you will talk to will tell you that they once believed in God as a child, or in a higher power that they associated as *love*. It wasn't until abuse of some sort entered their lives where they assumed there either was no God at all, or they ended up hating Him because He "allowed" these things to happen to them and did not come to help.

Life continued to go on and I was desperately trying to get on welfare and find housing. We went back to stay with Charles' mom once again until we got our own apartment in the U District. This did not last very long as Charles was always picking up women and bringing them home, expecting us to be some big, happy family. It was definitely not normal, as was nothing I had been doing in my life at this time. One of the girls had a pimp and he came and stabbed Charles with an ice pick forty times. He was lucky he lived through that event. I finally left that area because I did not want to prostitute myself anymore. I wanted to find a real job to support my son. I finally got on welfare and it was enough money for me to rent an apartment in the Capitol Hill area. It had horrible cockroaches, but it was my own place. I had a mattress on the floor and a little couch. Charles came with me and unfortunately, I was still dragging him around with me because I was all alone. I had no one else. I accepted all of the horrible things he did, because I just could not be alone. Fear encased my every decision, so I had to put up with whatever abuse life brought me; it was my own fault so now, I had to live with it.

Toxic behavior is not just something you can let go over night; for few maybe, but for many, almost impossible! We get stuck in patterns and cycles that drive us further and further away from not only our true selves, but also away from the arms of a loving God. We desperately need people in our lives that are firm with us, bold and unapologetic to call us out of darkness and into the truth and light of what we are doing to ourselves. This is not always easy to receive, but it is absolutely necessary not only for our emotional, mental, and psychological needs, but more importantly to save our lives… literally!

"Faithful are the wounds of a friend, But the kisses of an enemy a are deceitful" Proverbs 27:6, NKJV. (Thank you Julia, this was you in my life.)

Charles decided to become a Buddhist to get clean and sober. He had tried before to be a Catholic and other things, but this time, he had made a decision to study Buddhism. He had this Buddhist box and if you touched it or turned it around, he believed that it would mess his life up, or change it somehow. He was still staying out all night. I assumed he may have still been raping women, or something he should not be doing. I was mad at him because I was around six months pregnant and desperately needed him to help me raise this baby. I turned the box around three times, expecting something to happen good for him. I did not know what I was doing. I desperately wanted him to get clean and sober. I had this fantasy of having a wonderful life with my husband and our kids, which was never going to happen with this man. At this point, I was willing to do anything, no matter how strange, to get him to change.

I made a friend in our apartment complex with a woman named Barbara. She was actually friends with Charles. We would go to eat at an all you can eat salad bar up on Capitol Hill every day, so that I could eat enough for the baby. One day, Charles brought a young girl home, which he was still doing often, and he wanted us to have a threesome. Again, I was so desperate not to be alone, so I considered it, but I could not go through with it. I threw up all in the bed. He got angry with me and beat me up, eight months pregnant and began having sex with this girl in front of me. She was underage and he is so lucky he did not go to jail. Another time, he came home with another girl, and I got upset with him and he shoved me down the steps. I was probably around 7 ½ months pregnant at this time. I was now trying to figure out how I was going to get away from him and this lifestyle. Not Russell, not Derrick, and not Charles… not one of them was going to be a good enough person for me to live a good life. I was just so desperate that I would accept anything and anyone. I never felt worthy of anyone. I was a broken woman.

"I will praise You, for I am fearfully and wonderfully made; Marvelous are Your works, And that my soul knows very well" Psalm 139:14, NKJV.

My life was so chaotic for a long period of time. I did not blame my parents for not allowing me to come back home. They had enough chaos in their own lives for so long, they probably just wanted peace, and it was understandable. I didn't understand it then, but I do now. One day, I was on the bus going downtown to Nordstroms to get some stockings. They were so thick and warm, and I needed some. As soon as I step off of the bus, there were the Vice Cops. I was arrested again for violating probation. I am eight and a half months pregnant. I am about to give birth and here I am going to jail. The judge decided to be hard on me and gave me twenty-seven days because he was sick of seeing me violating my probation. So, I go to jail, probably around the 20th time for me, at this point in my life. I was scared to death that I was going to have my baby in jail. By the way, I was not even fully sure Charles was the father of my baby because I was turning tricks and I was with an Italian man around the same time, and the contraception failed. I was sick to my stomach; the worst thing ever for a prostitute. I did not know if I was going to have a biracial son with Charles, or with this Italian man. I was embarrassed and ashamed not knowing who my son's father was, and telling the doctors that I just simply did not know.

I am in jail and they put me in protective custody because I was pregnant. I read the Bible the entire time I was there. I don't know how much I actually got from that time, but I remember going to phone booths while prostituting and I would find a Romans Road tract, seeing someone share the Gospel on the streets, or seeing a nun coming up and praying for me. I always knew Jesus was around me through these people. Evangelism is very important. Though I remained in this lifestyle for quite some time, I knew that when I was ready, He would welcome me with open arms due to these precious people that shared the love of Jesus with us on those streets. In my darkest moments, there He was in a phone booth, or within a sweet little nun, or whomever He would send. Here I am in this jail cell thinking I am going to have this baby in this place, praying to God that I would not. I eventually got out, still pregnant. Thank God! I do believe He heard my prayers as I prayed every day that I would not have to have my son in jail.

I finally get home to our apartment on Capitol Hill, on Belleview and Denny, and I go into labor. Charles goes with me to the hospital but does not stay as he went to get high. He leaves me at the University of Washington Hospital in full on panic attacks and anxiety. I am nineteen years old, about to have a baby with a pimp, and all alone. I begin to go over my life and realize that I have never had someone to really love me. I sold my body for these men, gave them all of my money, did inexplicable things, was beaten and abused, and here I am having a pimp's baby. What kind of life would he have? Would he be like his father? Could I shelter him from the life I had chosen?

I was in labor, extremely scared but excited at the same time to be a mother. I believed God had sent me this son to save me from this life. This was a selfish motive for a mother, but it was my reality. He ironically saved my life, so I could raise him. I was in labor for 24 hours and nothing was happening. They gave me medication to induce but it was not working. After 48 hours, they decided that I would need a C-section, which was my worst fear. My anxiety was over the top, and anytime I was afraid or alone, I would tell funny stories or jokes or try, in some way, to get my mind back on track and get through it. I would be overly nice just to get myself back, and the nurses were very nice to me even though they knew I was a prostitute. They knew what I was going through and where I came from, but cared for me anyway. At 1:57am on May 19th of 1983, I gave birth by C-section to Elliot Mason Brady, my beautiful oldest son who turned forty years old this year.

He was a beautiful black baby boy, he was Charles' son. I was relieved that it was not the other man's baby. I did love Charles even though it was an unconventional lifestyle we were living. I believe he loved me in his own strange way. I don't believe he knew what real love was either through his own abuse and the demonic oppression he faced as a child. After Elliot was born, my mom and dad finally came up to meet him. It was my first visit where the idea was presented of maybe letting me come home. My brother also came home after almost fifteen years of being gone. Remember, he was the one that molested me as a child. I was excited to see him but it was awkward all at the same time. I guess he didn't really know the damage he had done to me. The abandonment is what hurt the most. I just wanted to hear him say he was sorry. So, when I saw him, I thought for sure he would make things right, but all he could call me was a *nigger-lover*. He didn't want to have anything to do with me. He really only came home to reconcile with my father, and they did to some degree. That was encouraging.

I felt so crushed. I felt that something was unfinished. I have forgiven him and moved on with my life from the sin he committed against me. He was extremely broken. Again, I don't know all that happened to him as a child. I know there was a lot of darkness in his life. At the age of thirty-eight, he was in a treatment program at the Union Gospel Mission. He was walking home one night and got himself some heroin. He overdosed and died. My heart grieved for him. Truly a sad ending to his life.

I want to leave you with the Parable of the Lost Son. No one, not one, is so far away that they cannot come home. He is able to heal and deliver each of us if we would just come to Him. He does not judge us, but loves us unconditionally.

"But when he came to himself, he said, 'How many of my father's hired servants have bread enough and to spare, and I perish with hunger! I will arise and go to my father, and will say to him, "Father, I have sinned against heaven and before you, and I am no longer worthy to be called your son. Make me like one of your hired servants."

"And he arose and came to his father. But when he was still a great way off, his father saw him and had compassion, and ran and fell on his neck and kissed him. And the son said to him, 'Father, I have sinned

against heaven and in your sight, and am no longer worthy to be called your son."

"But the father said to his servants, 'Bring out the best robe and put it on him, and put a ring on his hand and sandals on his feet. And bring the fatted calf here and kill it, and let us eat and be merry; for this my son was dead and is alive again; he was lost and is found.' And they began to be merry" Luke 15:17-24, NKJV.

Chapter 6

a New Chapter is Birthed

"This means that anyone who belongs to Christ has become a new person. The old life is gone; a new life has begun!"
2 Corinthians 5:17, NLT

My friend Rosemary moved up to Seattle. She lived near me, and I would go over there often to spend time with her. One day, I received a call that someone what threatening to blow up our apartment because Charles had robbed them of their drugs and money. I knew that it was time to get Elliot out of that environment. The last straw for me was one night when Charles was in the bathroom after coming home, our son was a newborn, and he was shooting up and missed his vein and blood shot out all over the bathroom. He could have really died at that point. I just knew I could no longer live in an environment with this man that was shooting heroin, robbing people, staying out all times of the night with women, and just chaos at every turn with our newborn son.

I had to get away from him. This baby meant everything to me and I was now sober. I wanted to change and be a better parent to my son, than my mom and dad were to me. I was going to do my very best to be a good mother to him. My parents finally agreed to let me come home. After what felt like a twenty-year span of time to me, I was finally going home. My father told me that I could only stay for thirty days. What he did not understand was that I was suffering and recovering from prostitution and being trafficked. It was a horrible life for me. I had very bad post-partum depression, along with just being depressed in general after all I had lived through up to that point. I was doing well, I made it through. I got an apartment after living at home for thirty days. I got a job at ADP doing key punching. I made enough money to support me and Elliot.

Here I was faced with being alone without a husband, or someone to help me care for my son, and I was severely depressed. I was going to AA meetings and parenting classes with CPS. I went to them asking for help in how to raise my son. They were not used to people coming to them for help, but coming to take kids away from their parents. I was always very resourceful. When I needed a way to survive, I would find a way, no matter what stress it caused or how hard it was for me. Things were starting to look up, even though I still suffered from anxiety, fear, and depression at times. I enjoyed being a mother to my son. Unfortunately, I found out that my son had speech and hearing problems. He couldn't talk like he was supposed to, and I was faced with taking him to specialists and speech therapy. I was still suffering from addictions, prostitution, and being at poverty level myself, while trying to care for my son who desperately needed me.

"Then Jesus said, "Come to me, all of you who are weary and carry heavy burdens, and I will give you rest. Take my yoke upon you. Let me teach you, because I am humble and gentle at heart, and you will find

rest for your souls. For my yoke is easy to bear, and the burden I give you is light" Matthew 11:28-30, NLT.

Many times, because we either do not have families that will support us, or close friends that want the best for us, we will try to do all of these things in our own power. We were never designed to do life alone, and we were also not meant to lean fully on ourselves for the help we so desperately need in this life. God wants us to come to Him, so He is able to comfort us and care for us in our time of need. I learned early on to manipulate every situation to survive, not because I wanted to hurt others, but because I needed help to survive that I was not able to get naturally, so I tried to make it happen for me and my kids. I am not proud of this behavior but I know it was simply a survival technique to stay alive. I am grateful I learned later on to trust God with all my heart and that I didn't have to manipulate to survive, that I was able to live in the Sunlight of the Spirit of GOD.

Eventually, I started going to night school to learn how to become a computer programmer. I knew they made a lot of money. I got my certificate and began my first job but realized I had made a huge error in judgment. I went to school for a year but ended up not being very good at it. I was looking more at the money than doing what I really wanted to do. Elliot and I finally got on the housing list for low-income housing. I met a neighbor who was living with a man named Perry. As time went on, he would approach me constantly to be with him and I really did not want to be with any man at that point. Unfortunately, through his persistence and my lack of discipline in my own life and standing my ground, I had sex with him and became pregnant. I could not believe I had put myself back in this situation. Doing the same thing over and over again and expecting different results is called *insanity*.

I eventually moved to another city, Beaverton, and got a new apartment and he came with me. I had given my life back to Christ at this time, but was not doing a very good job of walking in the right path, of course, still having sex outside of marriage. Old habits are truly hard to break. We decided to get married and began going to a Bible fellowship together in Hillsboro, Oregon where we were receiving biblical counseling before we got married. We finally got married and my mom and dad came, but my father was definitely not happy. You could see it on his face. My life was so-called getting *normal*, if you will. I was married, making friends at work, had a cute little duplex in Oregon, and we were going to have a baby. My husband eventually showed his true colors. He was a very violent man. He did not hit me, but he would come home from work in violent outbursts, breaking things and tearing up our furniture. He had horrific temper tantrums that were frightening.

"A wrathful man stirs up strife, But he who is slow to anger allays contention" Proverbs 15:18, NKJV.

My son and I would sit on the couch watching him throw fits and just hold hands. Elliot was still unable to talk so I don't know all that possibly happened to him in the care of my husband, at that time. He had a very harsh way of disciplining children that I was not in agreement with, and I did not want my son, or our new child, to be raised this way. During the pregnancy with my second son, Eric, my husband became even more violent and obsessive. He would isolate me in our home, and I could not drive due to my anxiety. That familiar spirit of fear crept back up in my life and brought so much stress upon me. Perry would yell and scream at me all the time, causing me to relive a lot of my past fears and anxieties. I was now totally dependent upon him, as I was with the others. He would yank the phone cord out of the wall, so I had no method or way to call anyone.

My kidneys began to fail during my second pregnancy and the doctors stated it was due to the stress I was enduring in my marriage. I was in and out of the hospital and my mother would come and get Elliot during those long periods of time to keep him safe. I was very appreciative to her. I never told her why, but I think she instinctively knew what was going on in my marriage. Remember, she was an abused wife, as well. I am sure she picked up on the signs. I was in the hospital four times with kidney infections and during the last four weeks of being pregnant, I had to remain in the hospital. This was good for me, so I did not have to stay with Perry. I gave birth to Eric on January 18, 1987, at 5:15pm in the Oregon Health Science Hospital up on the hill in Portland. It was during some sort of St. Jude festival at the hospital with Sammy Davis, Jr. Perry was there for the delivery but he was freaking out and causing me stress and anxiety, of course. My family did not come for this delivery. I cannot remember why, possibly me asking them not to due to my situation. Here I was again, a mother to another child. I was okay with having two kids, I believed I could handle it. They were my life now. My whole purpose in life was to take care of my children. Fear was my first and last emotion every day of my life from that point until I was well into my 40's.

"Children are a gift from the Lord; they are a reward from him"
Psalm 127:3, NLT.

Eric was born and he had a few issues that took him into the NICU for a little while. After his levels returned to normal, he was brought to me to begin breastfeeding him. His father fainted when he was born, which was funny. My parents and family finally came to see us and I was sensing some sort of normalcy at this point. We went home with Eric and introduced him to his brother, Elliot. Elliot gave him his first bottle and it was so sweet. I still have that picture today. Sadly, Perry did not like Elliot too much and was always doing things to scare him. One day, I came home from a well check up with Eric and found a bruise around Elliot's neck. I asked Perry what happened, and he said that he had made a superman cape out of a blanket and tied it around him, and it got stuck on something and it choked him. I did not believe him. I never left the kids home with him by themselves after this incident. I would take them to my mother's house if I needed to do something. I did not trust my husband.

He came in one night and was angry again, throwing tantrums. I stood with Elliot by Eric's crib to keep them safe. He told me to go sit down. I tried to get Eric out of his crib, but he would not let me. He began throwing books around Eric's crib, which could have hit him and hurt him. It was at this point that I had had enough. He began his job as a security guard and went to work, and I called the battered women's shelter, packed our things up, and they came and got me and the kids. He had my only car, so I needed to find a way to get it back from him. I stayed at the shelter and was able to get a restraining order against him. I was going to leave this man. We had gone to counseling, to church, and tried everything we could, but nothing was changing within his behavior. One time, we went to church and Elliot wasn't acting good enough for him and he shoved him down a flight of four stairs at three years old. I was so mad and took off my shoe and hit him. I was sick of him hurting my kids and had enough of him.

The shelter was okay, but there were so many regulations; several being that I could not breastfeed my baby due to the openness of the facility and I could not sleep with him, as his crib was in another room. This was very difficult for me. We began to try to get Elliot speech and hearing therapy again. Unfortunately, one day Perry ended up at the front door of the shelter demanding they give him back his family. Due to the breach in finding our location, they kicked us out of the shelter. No one was safe with him and his violent behavior. I ended up going to several other shelters trying to get away from him. Here I am with a newborn baby and a special needs child trying to figure out how to get through it all. It began affecting my children horribly.

We must understand that our choices in men, women, husbands, or wives not only affect us, but our children, as well. We cannot be selfish just because we are in a bad situation, or a tough spot. I am living proof that making decisions irrationally regarding relationships is detrimental not only to you, but also your children. These people can not only destroy your life physically, but they will also destroy you emotionally, mentally, psychologically, and spiritually for the rest of your life if you are not able to get help. Your children can and will suffer the consequences of your choices for the rest of their lives, as well.

Perry began going to counseling saying he was getting better and that he wouldn't do it again. Like most battered women, I went back to him and we got a new place. I was willing to try one more time. The first day back with him, he busts out my driver side window in my face. He was yelling at me asking me why I was causing so much drama in his life. He had violated his probation with this incident, and I helped him when I went back to him. This was violation five or six at this point. I went back into the shelter and they helped me file for divorce. On January 3, 1988, we had our divorce hearing and the judge told Perry that because he did not have a lawyer, he would have to get someone that would supervise his visits with his kids and he would have to pay them. The judge ordered us to meet that night to sign the paperwork. I told the judge that this was not going to work, but he did not listen. I could not pay a babysitter because I did not have any money, as I was living in the shelter.

I met him that night to sign the papers. He was drunk and very violent. He forced me into his apartment and raped me. I was devastated. This was my husband and I could not understand why he insisted on continuing to be violent towards me. I left and went back to the shelter, broken and alone. My children heard me crying from the other room, just as I had with my mother. My heart was broken and I was alone and terrified. I received a call from my mom saying that my father was dying of cancer, and had only three months to live. My entire life was crumbling around me again. About four weeks later, I find out I am pregnant again. After the last abortion, I was not going to take the life of another child, so I decided to keep the baby. Perry was sentenced to nine months in jail for the rape, though they called it a "violation of restraining order," because we were still married. It was still rape because I did not consent. I could not scream and get help, because my two children were in the other room and this would have affected them horribly.

I was devastated. My father was dying, I was getting a divorce, and I had two kids and one on the way. I knew I was not going to get any help from Perry financially. In thirty-eight years, I may have received thirty dollars from garnishment. Not another penny. The shelter we were now living in was in the basement of a church, which was sort of like an apartment. I was nervous and full of anxiety all the time. I was trying to bond with my children and make things as normal as I possibly could for them. Eric's crib was in the room with me this time and Elliot could sleep with me, so it was a little better for us. They let us stay there for a year and I applied for Section 8 and Welfare. About seven months into my pregnancy, I was approved and we moved into a cute little house in Northeast Portland. It was a three-story house and I think I paid around $150.00 a month, which was really good. I began to prepare our home to welcome our new baby. I was so excited that I was having a little girl. I had suffered so much, but God kept showing me bits and pieces of joy through it all.

"In his kindness God called you to share in his eternal glory by means of Christ Jesus. So after you have suffered a little while, he will restore, support, and strengthen you, and he will place you on a firm foundation" 1 Peter 5:10, NLT.

Elliot was finally talking. The speech therapy was really helping him and he was going to an early childhood education program for disabled kids. We got him the help he needed and he was finally beginning to thrive. Eric was starting to show signs of dysfunction from living in all of the shelters and going through all of that trauma. He had not received the proper nurturing he should have had as a baby. He began acting out. I couldn't take him to daycare because he was biting the other kids. It was obvious that the trauma had really affected my sweet little boy. My father died on Easter of 1988. I had taken me and the kids to the beach on vacation to get some much-needed rest and peace when I got the call that he had another six to eight months to live. I was now on a bus with my kids trying to get home, and did not make it in time. They called and told me that he had passed away. I was devastated and grieving. I did not get to say goodbye to him. I felt like I could feel his presence leave the Earth, if that is possible. I just knew something tangibly left me that day.

I finally gave birth to my little girl Elyse on October 24, 1988, at 2:20pm. My mom did not come to see us. She was pretty much done with us at this point. One mixed baby was acceptable, three was not. With my dad gone, I am not sure she cared about anything anymore; she was grieving her husband and that was very understandable. My sisters would still come to see me and the kids. I was now more determined than ever to make this work for me and my kids. I went to work and began taking care of my family. I was adamant that I would not live on welfare for the rest of my life, or teach my children that this was the way for them, either.

Seven days had passed since Elyse was born. It was Halloween night. I got all of them dressed up and went Trick or Treating. When we got back home, I was sitting on the couch and all of sudden, I heard a banging on the front door. It was Perry. Somehow, he found out where we lived again. I don't know how he kept finding me as I never gave him any of my addresses. He pulled his car up on my grass, I assumed to sleep in his car at my house, but he forced his way into my house demanding that I give him his two kids. I had to play his game so that he would not take the kids and run off. I was terrified. I began to bleed heavily, as I was still bleeding from the birth of my little girl. It was literally running down my legs, but he did not care. He put his hand in my chest like he was going to hit me and told me, "You are going to give me those kids!" I told him to give me a few minutes to get them ready, and I ran out the back door with them and got in my car, bleeding, full of fear but determined to save my children from this man.

I got away and drove to the police station. They came and took him away once again. He could just never do anything normally. It always had to be a threat or a demand. The judge would not even allow him to see our children unsupervised. They knew he was a danger to them. If a court of law saw this, then you know it was serious. It was not like I did not want my children to have their dads in their lives. It broke my heart that none of my kids had their dads. For Perry, he just could not get himself together long enough to be their dad. It was either his way or the highway. I had promised myself that I was going to give my kids a better life than I had, no matter what that meant or what sacrifice I had to make. I was going to give them a better life. As I was trying to do this, I had my own mental health issues going on. He was back in jail, so we were safe for a little while.

Chapter 7

Relapse

**"I don't really understand myself, for I want to do what is right, but I
don't do it. Instead, I do what I hate. But if I know that what I am doing
is wrong, this shows that I agree that the law is good. So I am not the
one doing wrong; it is sin living in me that does it."
Romans 7:15-17, NLT**

I

t became even more evident to me that I needed to take care of my
children, so I got a job at a book binding company when I was
pregnant with my daughter Elyse. Three days into the job when they
saw that my kids were biracial, the lady that was my manager
approached me and said, "Oh my God, look what you have done to
your kids!" I was confused, and I asked her what she meant, saying,
"What? What?" I wasn't sure what she was talking about. She meant the
color of their skin. So, instead of firing me because they were racist, they
said it was because I was pregnant. Thank God in the state of Oregon,
this is against the law. I filed a lawsuit against the company and won. I
got a little stipend for the three days of work and an additional
$25,000.00. The lawyer took most of that, or a good portion of it. I think
I got around $15,000.00. I took that money and opened up a Montessori
school in my house. I made a cute indoor park, and I bought all kinds of

things. I painted the house and bought cribs and beds for the kids, as well as desks to do their schoolwork. I set it up nicely. I hired two grandmas to come and help me watch the kids, so they could rock them and care for them. It was a good marketing tool to get clients to come as they wanted their children to be in a good environment.

I started a business and worked really hard. I was very good at it, but it started to affect my children. Elyse was not happy that the other kids were in her "domain," which is understandable. This was her home. Eric really had issues as there was just too much noise with kids in the house and he began to act violently towards the other children. I had to take my own son to daycare, while I was running one in my home just to be sure there was peace. The entire point was to have my kids home with me, but it was just not working out. I know that sounds strange, but I was a single parent and I had to support my family and do what was best for everyone. I was the only one bringing money into my home. We began going to therapy four days a week, one for each of us. Elliot was going to a special school to help him, and Eric would eventually begin to go to one to help with his anger, rage, and violent behavior. I really wondered if he was picking up the spirit of his father. Perry was a very violent and angry man. Though Eric was really young, he did witness a lot of his father's rage.

The truth is I was having a hard time dealing with three kids in a normal setting, but the daycare was just becoming way too much for me to handle. I was trying to stay off welfare and run this business in excellence to support my family. I finally met another man at an AA meeting, his name was Elston. He was probably the kindest man I ever dated. He never did anything to harm me, he never hit me or abused me. He was quiet and went to work every day. He did have a lot of kids, so he had to work hard to pay child support. He was a good man. He took care of his children, and mine; he was just a good person.

I had walked away from God again and was obviously not walking the Christian life. I believe I walked away because I had not truly been discipled. I was taught religion. I hadn't really learned to walk with Jesus. I didn't even know who He really was. I didn't know if I could even trust Him because I had not developed that kind of relationship with Him at that time. I was still going to therapy with the kids and going to AA every day. I had been sober for quite a while. Elston was working every day and helping us out in the home. He would help me clean and supported us as much as he could. He was a good friend. Unfortunately, he relapsed in his drug habit and began to steal things from me to pawn, but he would bring it back the next day and apologize to me. He pawned my video recorder for drugs and found a way to get some money to buy it back for me.

My life was spiraling once again, and everything was chaotic for me. I was trying to figure out how to navigate everything that was going on, but it was just getting worse. My children were not doing well at all. They were all acting out at this point. Elliot had to go and stay with my mom much of the time. Elyse was doing okay, but she had some rough patches, as well. Eric took the brunt of it all. He just could not cope with all of the chaos going on in our home. I could not simply stop working as I had to take care of my kids. I did not want to go back on welfare. It was just not my goal. For three and a half years of Eric's life, I tried really hard to help him work through his outbursts and behavioral issues. He would get so angry and bite children to the bone. He bit his sister's elbow to the bone one time and I had to rush her to the emergency room. She was still a newborn at the time. He would open up the door while we

81

were driving. I do believe he could have inherited the spirit of rage from his father, but I also believe that as we were jumping from homeless shelters, and running from his dad, he just simply did not get to bond with me as mother and son. His therapists called it a detachment disorder. But my dying love for this child just could not allow him to suffer any longer because of my mistakes and the sins of his father against this family. The therapists kept telling me that Eric needed a two parent, stable family, that he would never get well with me. I didn't listen to them, I was his mother; who better could love him but his mother. But how could I be so selfish? If Eric could have a better life, why wouldn't I allow him to? This decision weighed heavy on my heart daily and for the rest of my life. This precious, sweet little boy would be the heartbeat of my sorrow from the day he left until I saw him again many years later.

I did everything I possibly could do to keep my family together. I worked thirteen hours a day in the daycare, but it was taking a toll on my entire family. What I thought was a good idea by starting the daycare business, ended up in failure for me as a mother. Elston and I broke up, but he still came back and worked for me in my daycare, which was helpful. The kids really liked him so there was no problem there. Eric was still acting out. I met a friend from his school, a teacher named Audrey, who was working with Head Start. Eric fell in love with her and went to stay with Audrey and Michael a lot. Her mother worked in my daycare as one of the grandmas. Her name was Grandma Thelma. She was very sweet and funny, but she said things exactly how they should be said. She was very real. The daycare was beginning to take a hit due to the chaos. I was losing kids from the daycare and my focus was really on Eric at this point. His acting out was apparent and he needed help that I just couldn't figure out how to give to him. Eric was a sweet little boy and very loyal. He loved to sit with his momma and eat popcorn and watch movies with me. Even when I was in beauty school, I cut all his hair off and he did not get mad at me. He just said, "It's okay momma, you tried." He was full of life and personality. He loved his siblings, he was so loyal.

I eventually lost Section 8 and had to move in with another lady, and she had five kids. We had the second house where I ran the daycare business, but it was falling apart slowly. I was not sure what was going to happen with the daycare and just trying to figure out what we were going to do. Eric's therapist was very concerned about him and stated that he really needed a two-parent family, that I was not taking care of him. They convinced me that I should not be the one to care for my child because of my past trauma and childhood abuse, and that there should be two parents that would help him. I wasn't ready to accept the thought of giving up my child. Apparently, it came up that I was doing something illegal when I prepared my paperwork for the state every month regarding my business. I was oblivious to anything illegal, as I thought I was doing everything right and in accordance with what they told me. One day, there was a knock at the door of my daycare, and it was the Feds.

Elston answered the door and I ran out the back because I was terrified. They said they needed to see Mrs. Manns to go over the bookkeeping. I had no idea what was going on, but evidently, there was something off that I did not know about. My world was falling apart, once again. I went out with my girlfriend to a club one night, trying to forget all my problems and I met another man. His name was Michael. I had been sober and working hard to live a normal life and raise my kids the right way, but it was just so hard. I was so desperate for someone to help me not only raise my kids, but also to help me support them. I was looking to the world, instead of Christ to help me. I was about to learn some very hard lessons, once again. We hooked up and of course, as with all the others, I fell for him, which was my desperation all over again. He told me the only way that I could be with him was to leave the state and become a prostitute again. He did not want to be around kids and wanted me to change my entire life to be with him. Initially, I was not having it, but he kept pushing and pushing to get me back in this life.

"It's your sins that have cut you off from God. Because of your sins, he has turned away and will not listen anymore" Isaiah 59:2, NLT.

We cannot keep living in sin and expecting our lives to get better. I was running from God at this point because I was in and out of a place of seeking Him. I was making all kinds of excuses as to why I could not form a relationship with Him. Though I didn't know what love was, or what true relationship looked like, I still had an opportunity to surrender my life to Him and I chose to continue to live in sin. I was searching for others to fill the void in my life, instead of seeking the only One that was able to fill my every need.

One day, he said to me that if I could make the money now like I did when I first went into prostitution, I could keep my kids. I have to say, it was an interesting proposition. I was living in this visual reality which was not reality at all. I thought these were my only choices, but of course, they were not. I could have done many other things instead of going back into prostitution. Elliot was with my mom, Eric was still staying with Audrey, and I had Elyse with me all the time. I started to turn tricks again on the street. I went out one night and met up with a man on Sandy Boulevard. He pulled up in a car with a MADD (Mothers

Against Drunk Driving) sticker on his vehicle and he had a car seat in the back of his car. I got in the car and he began to drive pretty far away from where he picked me up. This doesn't usually happen with someone that just wants to turn a trick. We stopped and he parked the car near Burnside and immediately snatched me by the back of my hair and told me he was going to tie me up and take me to a warehouse in Clackamas and bring me back. The fear of God ran up and down my spine, I was terrified.

I thought for sure he was going to kill me. He told me that if I did what he said, he would take me back. I didn't believe him. I looked on his back seat and there was a body bag just sitting there. I sat there and pleaded with him that I had three babies at home, was a single mom, and I was just trying to make enough money, so we weren't homeless. I begged him not to kill me. He was calm and chillingly polite. It was eerily odd to me. He had automatic locks in his car, so I could not get out. He had a knife in his hand, and I said to myself, at least I am going to go out fighting because I was not just going to let him kill me. I tried to get out of the door and with him trying to stop me, he dropped the knife. I turned around and kept prying the door handle. I was just waiting to feel the warm sensation of a knife stabbing me, but it didn't. I kept shaking the door handle and finally, the lock popped open. That was my *Jesus Moment*. God got me out of that car. I grabbed my wallet and my purse, and I just ran as fast and as far as I could to the closest building, which was a 7-11 down the street.

I was screaming, "Rape, rape, rape..." I didn't know what else to scream. He is driving off with the car door still open. As I was running, I came up to a man that said to me, "Whore, shut up. No one is trying to hurt you." I kept running and got across the street to the 7-11 and there was an elderly homeless man sitting on the curb. I was crying heavily and told him that a man just tried to kill me in his car and pointed to where he was driving off. I asked him if he could walk with me to my car and he did. I told God at that moment if I ever got out of this life, I wanted to help the homeless.

I got home and I just could not believe what had just happened. I remember sliding down the back of the front door and just sitting on the ground shaking and shivering because of what just took place. Michael was nowhere to be found. When he came home, I tried to tell him what happened, but he simply did not care. That should have been my first clue to just leave him behind but of course, he kept manipulating me by using my kids as a pawn, telling me that I needed to do this for them. I thought if I could just find someone to keep my kids for a little while and go out of town to make enough money, I could come back and get them, get a house, and start another business. Well, that was unreasonable thinking because what I was doing was illegal and I was leaving with a man that was a crackhead, but I didn't know it at the time.

I found someone to take Elliot and Elyse, but I could not find anyone to keep Eric for me because of his behavioral issues. Audrey could not keep him. CPS and the other agencies had been hounding me for months about Eric, saying he needed a stable family environment. They had taken away Perry's full parental rights because he would not show up to any of the appointments. I did not know Perry's family to even think about asking them for help. Now, I wish I would have known them because I could have made the transition for Eric better. I probably could have gotten him back after I had straightened my life out. What I was about to do was single-handedly the stupidest decision of my entire life. It was a mistake that has lived with me every single second of every single day for my entire life since then. A pain so excruciating that my life ended that day; now, all I could do was help my children live.

"Wisdom is the principal thing; therefore get wisdom, and in all your getting, get understanding" Proverbs 4:7, NKJV.

Wisdom is truly one of the greatest gifts from God. Unfortunately, many of us do not seek wisdom in our decision making. In our own self-sufficient and self-reliant ways, we think we can live our lives how we want, choose to raise our children without the covering and shelter of God, and live outside of the boundaries of a God-centered life. Even the so-called happiest and most stable of families in the world, in our eyes, cannot be fully whole if they are not in relationship with the Creator of Heaven and Earth. Many believe they are wise and don't need God, oh how foolish they are, and will eventually see how much they do, indeed, need Him.

"What sorrow for those who are wise in their own eyes and think themselves so clever" Isaiah 5:21, NLT.

We went to a court hearing with CPS to figure out what was best for Eric. They weren't taking him, but they were trying to figure out what was the best placement for him. They threatened me that if I did not decide that day, that they were going to take him. I asked Audrey and Michael to keep Eric. They decided to adopt him and make it an open adoption, so we could still see him and he could come back home when I got myself together. This was supposed to be the easiest way for him to transition where it would not be traumatic for him, and he could still be with his family soon. I did not want to give my son away. I loved him with all my heart just like I do my other two children. The State of

Oregon promised me that if I gave custody to them, because they could not afford a private adoption agency, that they would approve of it. It was very hard, and it took me another six months to actually go and sign the papers for the open adoption.

As soon as I signed over custody to Michael and Audrey, the state reneged on their promise stating that they were a black couple, and that Eric needed a biracial family instead. Within thirty days, Eric tore up his adoptive parents' entire house. He must have sensed this was not the place he was supposed to be. He ended up in foster care for three years, which was never my goal, or desire, for him. My goal was to give him a better life, which was a selfless act because it was extremely painful for me. I was relapsing back into the life I tried to get away from, a place of utter desperation, depression, and suicidal thoughts. I was destroying my life because I felt like I had failed all my children. My life was over now... I was *dead*.

I fought through Perry. I fought through my mother and father. I fought through it all to get to this place. Elliot went to live with my mom. Elyse lived with Rosemary, and Eric was in a foster home. I was destroyed, heartbroken, and ready to die. I went back into survival mode. I called every Senator, Governor, and Attorney General I could find to get them to help me get my son back. I told them this was a planned event and that the State of Oregon was going to give Michael and Audrey temporary custody until I could get back on my feet, but that they lied and took my son. I remember laying on the apartment floor in Seattle crying for two days straight, not even able to get off the floor. Michael was sitting right there next to me but did not care whatsoever. It was all about money to him. I was working at a massage parlor down the street, and he was taking all my money.

I remember waking up one day and there was an eerie feeling in the apartment. I couldn't find Michael anywhere. His keys were on the couch, so I assumed he wasn't gone. I looked all over for him. I walked into the kitchen, and he was in the storage cabinet smoking crack. I was so angry with him. I told him he was the biggest idiot I had ever met in my life. I could not believe I had followed this man to Seattle from Portland to end up like this again, but I had no one and nowhere to go. I had lost my Section 8 housing, the house I lived in with the other lady, my job, and my son. I was at rock bottom once again. I continued at the massage parlor but was not making a lot of money. Michael was beating me, disrespecting me, cheating on me, and smoking crack and doing other drugs. I just brought the worst of the worst with me everywhere I went. I was in another prison. He told me I was the worst mother ever, and that my kids were lucky they did not have me in their lives.

"And what do you benefit if you gain the whole world but lose your own soul? Is anything worth more than your soul?" Matthew 16:26, NLT.

What is worth losing your soul over? What is worth losing your children for? What is worth losing your entire life to obtain? I had sold my soul, if you will, trying to give my kids a better life, but not understanding I was making their lives a living hell. Without the wisdom of God, I was paving a pathway to hell in my life and in the lives of my children. Please understand that there is absolutely *nothing* in this world that is worth losing yourself, your children, or your life for. The end will surely be destruction, take it from me.

A lot happened during this time. I worked in massage parlors from Federal Way all the way up to Everett. I worked in a massage parlor called K&C Spa when I first got to Seattle. The owner was a lady named Sonny, she was originally from Korea. She hated me and every other woman that worked for her. She was truly a trafficker. She trafficked Asian women from Asia with the mafia and brought them to the United States. It was horrible what she did to those women, as well as those of us that worked for her in the massage parlors. We would get a fee for giving the men a massage, and then we would ask for a tip from the men for "extra" services. She would take half of that and put it in an envelope in her safe. I worked with a lot of nice girls. We were all about the same age. We all got along good. I met this one girl that I love to this day. We have been friends for about thirty years; she came from Canada. We were both Catholic kids and came from some of the same experiences. She was my safe place; I trusted her. She was a good friend. She had a horrible pimp that threw her out of his car going around 60mph. She broke all her fingers on the freeway. She was finally able to get away from him, and we worked together in this same location.

Sonny, the owner, brought this one girl over from Korea. She would sit on the floor in a position that was normal for their culture, but she was rocking back and forth pulling her hair out of her head in clumps. It was clear that she was tormented. She was brought over here not of her own free will and forced to do horrible things to make this woman and others financial gain. We knew what was going on, but we stayed out of it because it was extremely dangerous. I learned more than I wanted to know about many of these men, their peculiarities, and their own sin. I fully understand that all of us have stories. All of us have pasts. All of us have sinned. My story is not to cast judgment on anyone, as I made the choice the prostitute my body. Yes, it was for survival, but it was still sin. The Bible clearly states the obvious:

"... for all have sinned and fall short of the glory of God" Romans 3:23, NKJV.

When you are being trafficked, or pimped, though you may have made the choice to work in this profession, you still feel victimized. It is a life for no one. There will never be a good end for anyone living like this. In fact, it is not living at all, but merely existing. There are things you will do that you would not otherwise do if you were not living as a prostitute, or in the streets, period. I can promise you that many of us that chose this lifestyle did not do so because we wanted to, but because we had to, in our eyes. Many of these people were sexually assaulted as children, physically abused by their parents, and saw things as children that no child should see. These people are broken and lost and fighting to survive in the darkness of these streets.

One night, me and this other lady were working together, and the owner brought in this Buddhist monk from Korea. The girl I was working with was high on heroin and going in and out. He was smoking and had a pig's head with him. They had prepared all this food for him and had a bowl of water outside for spirits and a fish over the doorway. She said that he was coming to ward off evil spirits and to bless her business and make it better. It was all very strange and scary for me. I was so scared they were going to do something to us or use us for a sacrifice or something. Seriously! Trust me, we saw things most people will never see in their lifetime.

A few weeks later, the massage parlor was raided, it was shut down, so I had to go work at a spa in SeaTac. We didn't make much money there like we did at K&C, it was horrible. So, I went to work at a spa in Burien for a lady name Carmen. All of her daughters were prostitutes, and her sons were pimps; they all lived a life of prostitution and trafficking. She played like a victim, but she was very manipulative. She was a gorgeous woman. I am not sure what ethnicity she was, but she was extremely beautiful. She approached me and told me that we should start our own massage parlor. I researched everything concerning starting a business, but she was the one that really opened the business. She just hired me and I worked for her. I made enough money to finally bring my children home with me. I got a nice apartment near Milton Lake.

It took me a while to get Michael out of my life. He would steal my car and leave me and the kids stranded for days. I had no family whatsoever. Holidays were horrible as we had nowhere to go, and no family to spend it with. Mind you, I came from a very large family with six brothers and sisters, and my parents did, as well. So, I have a lot of cousins, aunts, and uncles, but not one would have anything to do with me and my kids. This life carries with it many struggles. It was devastating.

I learned something very valuable in a sermon a while back that said, "You can pick your sin, but you can't pick your consequences." People were sick of the drama that I kept falling into and the choices I was making due to a life filled with trauma. The devil was destroying me and I was letting him. I thought I was smarter than him, making the same decisions over and over again, hoping it would be different each time.

I ended up getting arrested at *Carmen's Touch*, the massage spa where I was now working. That began the end of me there. I had gone to massage school so that I could be licensed in the locations. They pay you more when you are a licensed professional or a prostitute, essentially. I got my license taken away from me because I had a prostitution charge. I paid to get it back, but then got arrested again and got it taken away permanently. This was my circle of life. These patterns just followed me for such a long time. It was second nature to me. I worked for Carmen for about a year and the things that went on and the extra things I had to do for these men, aside from the massages, was horrible. I just remember sitting in the room one day crying profusely. The Bette Midler song, "Wind Beneath My Wings[1]" came to my heart. One part of the song states, "Did you ever know that you're my hero?" I was looking for a hero to come and rescue me. I knew Jesus, but I didn't *know* Jesus. I didn't really know His character and I certainly didn't think He loved me because I was wretched. I didn't have enough of the Truth of the Word of God within me to know all of that was a lie.

I remained in this state for so long because I felt like I deserved it. Look what I had done to my children, my family… everyone I ever came in contact with in my life. We lost our home again, as well as my job… one again. The cycles were never-ending. So, we decided to go up North and ask my mom if she would help me open a massage parlor, and she did. She helped me get everything together and paid for all of what was needed to get it started. I put my name on it and Michael came and stole every penny that I made from that location. I then learned how to gamble because I was getting very desperate. I was playing poker and bingo, which was a way to make money so I wouldn't have to turn tricks again. No one really makes money in a casino, except the casino, so I began making crazy decisions. I was on the suicide track for real.

---

[1] Midler, Bette. "Wind Beneath My Wings." Beaches, 1st ed., Atlantic Records, 1988, Track 2.

One day, the license inspector showed up to the massage parlor from Snohomish County. He told me that I was in violation and that I needed to pay him right there. He wasn't talking about money, because the other Korean owners said they had already paid him. I told him I was not going to "pay" him. I did have a little bit of integrity when it came to myself, but it didn't do me any favors because in thirty days, I got raided. I was probably the shortest-lived Madame in the United States. I was sitting there on Super Bowl Sunday in 1994 and had just gambled all of my money that I had made that day.

Next thing you know, I am in handcuffs pleading with the cops not to charge me with promoting prostitution. My mom did all of this for me to get the shop set up, paying her hard-earned money to help me, and I screw it up again. Literally, as I am in handcuffs, we had a small earthquake in South Everett, Washington. Only in my life would this happen, God was not happy with me.

They did not arrest me and told me that they were not going to charge me right away. I wasn't promoting anyone, my pimp was, and I did not have any girls working for me at that time. They were going to charge me with promoting prostitution. No matter how many times we purpose to change the trajectory of our lives, unless we first separate ourselves from the toxic and unhealthy environments, including people, and two, purpose to substitute those destructive habits with positive and healthy conditions and relationships, we will continue to relapse and fall right back into those same dark cycles, patterns, and pits again. Not one of us is above falling into temptation, but if we will heed His wisdom in the Word of God, He can and will lead us on the path to freedom.

"No temptation has overtaken you except such as is common to man; but God is faithful, who will not allow you to be tempted beyond what you are able, but with the temptation will also make the way of escape, that you may be able to bear it" 1 Corinthians 10:13, NKJV.

Chapter 8

A Good Man Falls 7 Times

**"The godly may trip seven times, but they will get up again.
But one disaster is enough to overthrow the wicked."
Proverbs 24:16, NLT**

I was looking at five to ten years in prison for promoting prostitution, even though I was the one being prostituted. My pimp was let go because my name was on the business, not his. He had physically and sexually abused me and took every penny from the business as well as my expensive car and left me there with no way to get home. After he saw the money drying up because I could no longer work and was looking at prison time, he became extremely violent. He picked up a T.V. turner and hit me in the face with it right on my cheek bone in front of my children. I usually just let him beat me up. I was not a fighter, plus I was deathly afraid of him. This time, I had had enough. I stood up and I picked up this stand-up lamp and began bashing him with it. I lost it! I was losing everything and was about to take a felony for this man. I had to sell the business because I had gambling debts to the mafia. The casino owner came over to my business with five of his men. I was scared to death, and thought they were going to kill me. Michael did not care. If he got what he wanted, which was money, he did not care what happened to me.

The next morning, I woke up and he was gone. He had stolen my car and left the state for Portland. I was livid! I had to call my mom to get help. She was an enabler for me, but I was also a liar. I did not tell her all that was happening, so it was not her fault. I asked her to pay the rent so we would not get thrown out on the streets. I contacted a program called *Up & Out*, run by Jody Davis and she came to help me. I also had a counselor come and see me from a program called *One Place*, it's a school for homeless children when their parents are in shelters.

An angel came into my life at this time named Jean. I did not know at the time that she was dying of leukemia. She would come to my house with a pimp living with me to counsel me and my kids, encouraging me to leave him and go back to Portland to a program she had found for us. She was even willing to pay to get us there. Of course, this took place before I was raided so I could not leave due to the legal situation I was facing. I was losing my mind at this point. There is a lot I do not remember from this time because I had gone through so much trauma, but I could not blame anyone but myself because I made these destructive choices over and over again. I could not blame my family for not wanting to be a part of my chaotic life. We grew up with enough chaos in our own home. They didn't want or need any more confusion in their lives. It was better for me that strangers helped me when I needed it. This did not take away the pain, loneliness, sadness, and rejection, which I faced every day of my life for probably thirty-eight years.

"For the whole law can be summed up in this one command: "Love your neighbor as yourself" Galatians 5:14, NLT.

From the Green River to the Lily of the Valley

I eventually got my car back from Michael. I didn't have any money to get back home. I convinced my mother to let me move back in with her, but she did not want it to be for long. At that point, I was in desperate need of treatment after all I had endured during those seven years of being away in Seattle again. Jody Davis was another angel that God sent to help me. She rented a U-Haul, helped me pack up all my stuff, and drove me to Portland. When I got back home, my mother was horrible towards me. She would hide behind doors saying she was scared of me. There was a paranoia she was experiencing that was extremely weird to me. I was still Susie, but I was a *broken* Susie. I wasn't going to hurt her, steal from her, or do anything that would harm her. She lied to my family and told them that I had taken money from her, that was never true. She would give me money to help me. Was I always completely honest about what I did with the money, no I was not. I was in survival mode from one day to the next trying to stay alive with my children. Trying to dig my way out of the hole I had made.

I eventually got a job working at Pepsi as a dispatcher. They fired me after two weeks because I was too emotional. My life was chaotic and I was in desperate need of professional help. My mother was calling me constantly stating that my kids were out of control, and I just simply could not function. There was just no help for me there where I could get the kind of support I needed to get out of the kind of life I was living in. Again, I blame no one but myself and my mom did so much for me when she did not have to, but I know it was mostly for my children. I still had a very bad gambling addiction, but there were not many places to gamble in Portland like there was in Seattle. I was so desperate for money, once again, and found a program back in Seattle that would pay my rent for me. All I had to do was pay my utilities, so I found another job close to the apartment I had found. I was finally away from Michael, at least for now.

One night, I woke up to the Psychic Network Hotline on television. Dionne Warwick was on their singing something, and the story was showing a family that said they found their biological nephew through the Psychic Network Hotline, and they won $36,000 for being their 1st place winner of how this psychic network can help you. All of a sudden, I saw this little boy waiving, and it was my son, Eric. The devil tried to make a joke out of my life, but God in His wisdom, His kindness, and His mercy did not make me, or Eric suffer any longer. He let us find one another. Immediately, I knew he was with my ex-husband's family. They did not find their biological nephew through the Psychic Hotline because I married their brother and Eric was born during my marriage. I have forgiven them, but this was a very difficult time in my life.

I immediately called my ex-husband's mother and she gave me his brother's phone number. I contacted him and he cussed me out right away saying he was not going to let me talk to Eric. He told me he was acting really bad and talking to me would make it worse. I begged him to let him talk to us, that his brother and sister needed to know him. He judged me and told me that I was horrible for giving him away. He did not know all I had been through at that time, so I do not blame him for believing the way he did. He didn't know the depths of my situation and why I made the decision to give him up. It was for Eric. It was for him to have a better life. I made a selfless decision. I could have taken him with me to Seattle and made him run through that horrible lifestyle with me. Eventually, they did let me talk to him, but it affected him greatly. I did not like what he was going through, and they called me crazy. Yes, I may have been a little crazy, but more than that, I was extremely broken, but now I knew where my child was. My heart was relieved. Eric was in a good place and he was safe.

I met a third angel whose name was Teresa; I met her in an awkward way. My daughter shoved her daughter off a swing and she came to my door to tell me. I told her I was sorry. Our kids were six years old at the time and now they are thirty-five and still friends. We became friends. She was struggling bad, too. She had a serious accident on my birthday a year prior that left her with a brain injury and she was drinking to cope with it at that point. I was still in AA trying to start over. We would help each other. She would keep my kids and I would watch hers. She would give me cash to help me out. She had this big lawsuit that she received and was just very generous. I fell in love with her mother and brother, and they invited us to Christmas dinner and Thanksgiving. We became a family. I appreciated her so much.

We would go to the ball fields together and to AA functions. I struggled to deal with life because of the trauma and because of my weight, too. I was obese. This was one way I could stay away from prostitution. I figured if I gained weight, no one would want me. The thoughts in my head were so out of whack and the lies I listened to and told myself led me to do some stupid things. I began gambling again, playing poker and bingo, wagering my entire welfare check away only to go back and beg my poor mother for more money. I am very ashamed of the way I manipulated my mother into giving me money due to my constant addictions. She decided to give me my inheritance while she was alive. I don't think she wanted to tell anyone that, but she told me that at one point. So, she did; one little piece, one meal, at a time. She did help me because of my kids and the situation I was in. I will forever be eternally grateful for all my mother did for me and my children. She is the reason I was able to begin getting well. I am sorry that her helping me hurt my sisters. That was not my goal; my goal was simply survival from a horrible amount of bad decisions.

So, I kept working and worked for about a year and then pumped up my resume. I got a better job and became a credit manager in collections for a corporate company. I built up my resume even more and obtained a higher paying job at another credit company with a bonus. By Y2K, I got picked up by a large internet company that had seven business models within their corporation as their corporate credit manager. I was making more money than I ever had in my entire life. I was working 12-13 hours a day. It took me two hours to drive to and from my job. I had a bit of agoraphobia all my life, and I would get extreme anxiety driving home at night. I would drive on the back roads all the way home. One night, when I got back to Seattle from Portland, I was driving in the wrong lane. I did not know I was not supposed to; I was ignorant of this, and I was pulled over by the cops. I had a warrant out for my arrest due to the pending charges of promoting prostitution I previously had working at my massage parlor. They told me it was a third-degree promoting prostitution charge, a Class C felony. It was a lower felony, but still one that could land me in jail for five to ten years if convicted.

I was devastated! Here I was starting over, thinking I was turning my life around and this came back to bite me. It had been almost a year and I thought they had thrown it out. I was checking from time to time, but nothing showed up. It must have all gone through around that time. My angel Jean, who had come into my life, lost her battle with leukemia, and passed away. She left me a card that said, "Spread your wings and fly with Jesus." There was another woman that came into my life, a counselor, and a psychotherapist, named Barbara Bennett. Her husband was a pastor, and they helped the homeless and were just kind and compassionate people. She helped me to understand that the anxiety I had had all of my life was spiritual. Partly chemical, but mostly spiritual. They would drive with me from Federal Way to Everett to all the court hearings.

The morning of my trial, I woke up and my daughter found a mood ring on the playground. She said, "Mommy, I want to give you this ring. I know you are going to come home in a little while." I got in the car crying. My son was looking at me very distraught. He was so angry with me. He had seen all that I had gone through with the bad decisions I had made over his lifetime, digging myself deeper and deeper. On this day, I was terrified. I was sure I was going to get convicted and end up in prison for five to ten years. We got to the court and the judge was a sweet man. I was convicted, but my sentence was not to go to prison, but community service. The judge pulled me up out of my chair and took me into his office. He told me that there are men out there that want to kill me. He said, "You are going to die out there if you keep up this lifestyle." He told me that he was letting me go on community service because I was a mother and told me to go home and do the right thing, or I would be going to prison.

I was so grateful. I knew this was God. My angels drove me back home to my children. I hugged them so tightly. Unfortunately, it left me with a felony on my record and a very bad one at that. It would not allow me to work at certain places, or with certain people. I began my 700-hour journey of community service at a library in the area and I had a DOC officer. It was scary. I was a felon. I was now the perpetrator. I had been the victim my entire life, but now I am the bad guy. My pimp got off scott-free and never paid for anything he did to me. In early 2000, the law changed on my crime. Because a pimp forced me to open a business in my name that was promoting prostitution and I was not promoting anyone to prostitute, nor did I receive funds related to the promotion of prostitution; the law now recognizes me as the victim, not the criminal. I never had my felony overturned, but in my heart, I am free of that crime and have been forgiven by the law and the Lord, Jesus Christ.

I began my new journey seeking out Jesus again. I looked to Teresa's mom Jan, my *adoptive mother*. She would watch Jan Crouch on TBN. I would go over to her house everyday while she held my hand and I cried. I would cry and cry and cry. I was trying to heal from all the trauma and depression I had gone through over the last fifteen years. By this time, I was thirty-three years old. It was monumental for me knowing that Jesus left this Earth at the age of 33, that He died, rose, was seated at the right hand of the Father, and that He left us with His precious Holy Spirit. He left us His Word of Truth. God was showing me that it was all about Him. I started going to a church down in Puyallup. The problem was that I did not feel like I belonged. I was very sensitive and anything anyone said to me, I became offended. I felt that no one liked me. I felt completely alone and rejected by the world, so I was not able to receive from anyone at that time. I did not last too long in many places. The people seemed a little too "normal," and I was certainly not normal.

I didn't know at this time that we all have sinned and fallen short of His glory (Romans 3:23). I didn't know concerning Ephesians 2:8, which states:

"God saved you by his grace when you believed. And you can't take credit for this; it is a gift from God."

I was just not aware of these concepts and principles in the Word of God. I had given my life to Jesus many times over, and was baptized just as many times, but I was not discipled. Many of the churches I attended were nice and had a lot of events, but they did not disciple people. I am not judging, just saying it was not available in the churches I attended. I am giving you an idea of why my life continued in destructive patterns due to me not being transformed by the renewing of my mind through discipleship. I continued building my career and eventually, I let Michael come back. Surely, it was the worst decision of my life. He promised me he would never hit me again and that he would not steal from me, either. I was lonely and wanted a man in my life. This destructive pattern went on until I was around 39-40 years old, so around the next seven or so years on and off. He was not living with me but visiting from time to time. I kept him at bay as much as possible.

I had gotten my daughter Elyse enrolled in a Soccer program where she thrived. My son Elliot was boxing at this time, but eventually began getting caught up with gangs, and doing and selling drugs. This would go on for the next seven years and he got into a lot of trouble. Elyse was doing well, but she was never able to truly trust or communicate with me, which was completely understandable. I had put a wall up around myself and shut almost everyone in my life off because I did not trust anyone. My depression was getting worse by the day. I should have been on medication and in professional therapy. I did share my life openly with some people that I met, just to get it off my chest. I also got some sort of therapy through Valley Cities. It wasn't great therapy, but it didn't heal the agoraphobia and anxiety.

I met a wonderful friend named Robin Wiebe who I love to death and she was another Angel in my life. She has a ministry called *Step by*

Step where she helps young women who are pregnant to not have to abort their child. She helps them to get the things they need and to counsel them to successfully have their baby, whether it is through adoption or keeping their child. It is a wonderful program. She was a licensed counselor and would come see me in her car with her newborn child and sit with me and walk me through my depression.

We were able to reconcile with Eric when he was around twelve years old. My friend Terry took me and Elyse to the airport to pick him up. I hadn't seen my son since he was three years old. I cannot fully explain to you what that felt like. I had spent so many years crying, praying, shaming myself, and feeling guilty for giving him up for adoption. I felt so low as a mother and a human being because what I thought was going to be a good thing for him was completely botched up by the state and others. I just wanted him to have a good life. Here I was, seeing my little boy for the first time in nine years. He came walking up the escalators and looking at his little face, he looked just like his sister. I gave him a big hug, but he was very mad at me. He thought that I had thrown him away.

We had these little visits throughout his teenage years. I would try to buy his love by getting him clothes and retelling the story repeatedly, trying to get him to understand. He couldn't. He did not understand that I had an abusive husband that would chase me and my kids around town all of the time, and that my life was in turmoil. He remained angry with me for a very long time. This was devastating to me, and one of the reasons I remained in depression for so long. I had waited so long to reconcile with him, only to have him hate me. All I wanted to do was to bring my family back together again.

Chapter 9

The Bottom of the Pit

"He will redeem his soul from going down to the Pit, And his life shall see the light." Job 33:28, NKJV

It was 2001 and I was working at Food Services of America when 9/11 happened. It was such a tragedy for the entire world. I was making good money, but eventually left this job and got unemployment. We lived in a house on Military Road at that point, and again, I was just trying my best to give my children a normal life, well as normal as possible. I was still battling with depression, anxiety, and fear, and I was still struggling with gambling and compulsive overeating. Years after my encounter with the Green River Killer, I would call back to King County every couple of years, and the Task Force would contact me, as well. I wanted to know if they had identified my friend Sandra Majors and if her family had buried her. I had given them her real name and the state where she was born. I had been praying that they would find her family and rightfully name her, and give her a proper burial.

Having been a prostitute and being around several of these women that were murdered, was hard for me. Sandra was an African American woman, so I feel like a lot of attention was not given to her case like so many of the others. No one really cared, but I cared. For thirty-four years, this stayed with me. They had yet to catch the Green River Killer, Gary Ridgway, at the time of my calls to them. I was completely obsessed with this case, and my daughter would always tell me to stop and let it go. I couldn't. I understood clearly that I had gotten away from this man, while two of my friends, fellow prostitutes, were murdered by him. Finally, November had come around and we were watching television and breaking news came on saying that they had arrested Gary Ridgway, the Green River Killer, after twenty years! I began screaming to the top of my lungs. It was like I was having a post-traumatic stress meltdown.

I sat on my bed weeping beyond explanation. They had finally caught this man that had murdered close to one hundred women, that he confessed to killing. He was only convicted of forty-nine of those murders. The fear and torment of all those years came rushing out of me. Those spirits had tormented me for so many years. Come to find out, this man was living not too far away from us. He had lived in several of the same places we did, while we were living there. At least part of that chapter in my life was laid to rest, but I was never going to fully rest until I knew that they had found, identified, and buried my friend, Sandra. That sweet little girl that danced with me on that corner, who was illiterate, she could not read or write, who was being beaten by her pimp that brought her all the way across the country, deserved to be recognized as a human being. My heart was aching for her. I wanted justice for Sandra Majors.

My son, Elliot, was hanging out with more dangerous people. He could not hold a job and he was barely going to school anymore. He did eventually graduate high school, but his life was spiraling out of control. I found a gun in his room, and he was drinking heavily. I knew he could not remain in my home around my twelve-year-old daughter. If someone found out, they would have taken her from me. He was so angry with me for not being in his life when he was little, as he was with my mother most of the time. My pastor suggested that I had to give him some ultimatums, or I would have to put him out of the house. He did not listen, of course, and eventually, I had to tell my son to leave my house. About three weeks afterwards, Elyse and I were coming home from Bible Study, and we heard loud sirens. We lived in a pretty quiet cul-de-sac, so we usually did not hear a lot of noise. We went to bed and around 2:30am, we were awakened by the King County Sherriff at our door with K-9 dogs. I am freaking out asking what was wrong. Immediately, I look at the officer and asked, "Is my son dead?" This was always my greatest fear. He told me no, but that he had shot someone. I asked if the other person was dead and he said no, but they were looking for my son.

The child was twelve years old, and my son was eighteen. He called me while the police were there and I told him not to go anywhere but wait for me so I could get a lawyer. There was a manhunt going on for him. My fear was that if they caught him, they were going to kill him because he was African American. I finally got in touch with a lawyer, and he advised me to turn him in. Elliot eventually came home, and I convinced him to let me turn him in, so he would not be harmed. I often wonder what really happened, as he was in the car with three other boys. The boy he shot, though he was twelve, was over six feet tall, so I am not even sure Elliot knew he was that young. He was a gang member, as well. It was a gang-related shooting. My son was convicted and went to prison for four and a half years. I was devastated.

I had finally let go of Michael, my oldest son was in jail, my youngest son hated me, and my daughter was not living right either. I didn't find out until ten years later all that she had gone through. My family was broken. We were traumatized by the lifestyle I had chosen to live for so many years. Strangely enough, my recovery process was probably the most damaging to and for us all. I really did not have a therapist or someone to help me walk through all the horrible memories and trauma I faced in my life. Gambling was my way to cope with all of this, but it brought on even more chaos in my life because if I didn't win, I would go home yelling and screaming at my kids. I did such horrible things that I regret to this day due to my anger. I am surely not making excuses, because I have lived with guilt and shame my entire life. I still have a son to this day that blames me and brings back up all that took place over thirty-four years ago. It is truly a hard burden to bear, but it is mine to bear, as these are the consequences of my own choices. As I was writing this book, my child forgave me and told me his childhood, although traumatic initially, when he lived with his aunt and uncle, was a good childhood. I was so grateful that all of my suffering had some good results for my child. I love him so much.

God is strong enough within me to let me know I am a new creation in Christ now. I know I have been forgiven and all my past sins have been wiped away. I simply must trust God that He will draw my children to that same place in their own lives. Not only were they traumatized by my lifestyle choices, but they also did not have a bond with my family. Every holiday, my mother would tell me we were not invited pursuant to my sister's request. I honestly don't know how true this was, but this is what she told me. I could not blame anyone for not wanting to be around us based upon my choices. I am sure they were concerned about their safety and possibly the safety of their own children. Living a life of a prostitute brings with it very dangerous people, not to mention the drugs and the gambling. They also never had any male upbringing. None of them had their father in their life to guide them or lead them as fathers should lead their children. They had no sense of security whatsoever. I cried every single holiday, which was even harder on my kids.

My children never got to be children. They were never able to do the things I did as a child like drinking hot cocoa, going to look at Christmas lights, and the childlike imagination of waiting for Santa and the excitement of it all. Their lives were burdened and darkened by my lifestyle, and I can never tell my children enough how very sorry I am for what I did to them. I will continue to do so until I breathe my very last breath on the face of this Earth. Unfortunately, due to the shame and guilt, I took on another addiction, which was compulsive overeating. So many would say such horrible things to me, but in my mind, I did not care, because I was doing the same things to myself. I was broken within because I had promised my first son that he was going to have a much better life than I did. That was a lie. Because I had not healed from what my parents did to me, I, in turn, did the very same things, if not more, to my own children.

"For he issued his laws to Jacob;
he gave his instructions to Israel.
He commanded our ancestors
to teach them to their children,
so the next generation might know them—
even the children not yet born—

and they in turn will teach their own children.
So each generation should set its hope anew on God,
not forgetting his glorious miracles
and obeying his commands.
Then they will not be like their ancestors—
stubborn, rebellious, and unfaithful,
refusing to give their hearts to God." Psalm 78:5-8, NLT

Generational curses are very real. If we do not raise our children in the Lord, and teach them His ways, they will assuredly walk in many of the same paths we did, or do. My father was a gambler, and my grandfather was, as well. My father married my mother and had a beautiful wedding, and came up to Seattle from Portland for their honeymoon. He gambled all their money and did not have any money to pay for their hotel room. They had to sleep in their car on their honeymoon. I come from a family of addicts. Alcoholics, gamblers, manipulators, dishonest people... sinners. I was now at one of the hardest crossroads of my life, because I was about to transition in major ways. I had finally left prostitution for good, and was working hard to support my children, but I was still broken and full of shame and guilt. I was sitting on my couch one day, and I cried out to God. I said, "GOD, I NEED YOU! I don't know who You are. I don't know how to achieve Your love, but I need You!"

I am forty years old at this time. I had been walking in and out of churches for about six to seven years. I was not submitting myself to anyone or anything, and not being discipled. I was still putting work first and my kids first, but that was just a part of my reality. We were poor and I needed to take care of my children, but I knew in my heart that something had to change in me, first. My daily life consisted of depression, anxiety, anger, and fear. There was no hope for my future, in my eyes. I was gaining weight extremely fast. I was a magnet for anyone that wanted to harm me or abuse me. I had no love for myself, so you could just look at me and tear me down, but I would still let you in my life. I did not think I deserved any better. I would accept anyone just so I would not be alone.

While in AA, I did learn that I needed to get to a place of seeking forgiveness and asking for forgiveness. That really did not take place until I finally stopped gambling. I have asked for forgiveness from all my children, and I have lived making amends before them for over twenty years now. I understand that if they still do not forgive me at this point, all I can continue to do is love them and pray. Again, you can pick your sin, but cannot pick the consequences of your sin. Sometimes, your sin can leave you without your family. And it did for me. I did not have my sisters, and me and my mother were just co-dependent upon one another. There was no real relationship with her, just a constant depending upon her when I was in bad situations. She would call me horrible names and I believe she was just utterly disgusted with me. One time, she came to visit me and took all the pictures of my daughter Elyse and threw them away, stating that I treated her better than Elliot. This was simply not true. I loved all my kids the same. Elyse was the only one that came around the time I was trying to make a better life for my family, so she came in a transition period.

I was trying to give her some stability and some normalcy in her life. The same friends and the same schools, so she could grow up with some sense of steadiness in her life. I believe I achieved that for Elyse. She eventually moved as far away from us as she could get, but I understood that she needed to find her own life and her own happiness. I have given all my children to God. A good friend of mine, Julia, told me that a pastor once told her something so powerful, and she share it with me. She said, "God loves your children more than you do." I thought, if God could love my children more than I do, which is a lot, then I had no other choice than to give them to Him. I was never going to recreate "The Brady Bunch". We were never going to have this "perfect, let's have Christmas and Birthday parties" kind of lifestyle. We hadn't formed any traditions as a family and this broke my heart for my children.

I learned that broken people, break people. I wasn't well enough to be a mother. Yes, God gave them to me, but I was not able to give them the kind of lives they deserved. After I put Eric up for adoption, I felt like Elliot and Elyse both deserved a better family, as well. I sent their pictures to the adoption agency and the lady told me, "Sorry, but biracial children are not adoptable." I was shocked! This was around 1980 or so. I thank God it did not go through. I don't think I would have made it without my babies. I am not sure I would be here today. I did love them dearly, I really did. I just could not seem to pull myself out of this depression.

I was now about to find Jesus for real. From the ages of 20-38, I was baptized at least seven times. I had accepted Jesus more times than I can count, but I was missing something. I was not being discipled. I really needed pastors to hear me, and hear me clearly; people need to be discipled! You cannot just open a church on Sunday and hope you have a bunch of functional middle-class people that are going to tithe and serve in your beautiful little ministry. No, you must disciple people. Jesus never walked alone; He had twelve disciples with Him. He discipled them, and they went and discipled others. He trained them, and they, in turn, went and trained others to do the same. This is almost non-existent in the Church today, which is mostly ran by one lone man, or woman, and most people just sit in the pews all their lives with little or no discipleship, at all. People need to be taught what it really means to be Christian. They need to know how to love God with everything within them, and to love their neighbors.

"And you shall love the Lord your God with all your heart, with all your soul, with all your mind, and with all your strength.' This is the first commandment. And the second, like it, is this: 'You shall love your neighbor as yourself.' There is no other commandment greater than these'" Mark 1:30-31, NKJV.

When you are broken and you have lived the kind of life I lived, worldly therapy does not work. I tried tapping, EMDR, and tried some kind of timeline mapping where you write down a timeline of events in your life and repeat them over and over again. All this made me more scared, more angry, more anxious, and more alone. Those were the spirits that followed me my entire life. I look at pictures of myself when I was younger, and it is obvious that I was severely depressed. My daughter would get so upset with me because I would not go on medication. She had a lady that was our neighbor try to urge me to go to the doctor. So, I went and this doctor encouraged me to get on antidepressants. I was livid! I did not spend twenty years of my life trying to get clean and sober for some doctor to tell me to medicate myself.

Depression is not necessarily always a chemical imbalance. You can go to the Mayo Clinic and read about it. I am not a doctor, but you can go and research for yourselves. From their observation, there are only two mental health diagnoses that need medication. One is schizophrenia and the other is bipolar, because both alter the chemistry in your brain. This is simply my own opinion, and honestly the opinions of many others, but I believe that all these mental health diagnoses that these pharmaceutical companies are pushing are demonic presences that need to be healed and removed in our lives. How? By the power and the blood of Jesus Christ! Again, I am not a doctor or a psychotherapist but every "therapist" I ever went to, I was analyzing them and knew that what they were offering was not helping me.

I was completely over the system. The police would not help me when I was being abused, trafficked, and strung out on the streets. The therapists would tell me I was crazy and making things up. The doctors wanted to medicate me, so I could not gain my true freedom. The system is not designed to help you; it's set up to enable you. Welfare and all of these systematic things are not there to help you, but hinder you.

Listen, I am not a professional and I surely do not have it altogether. My speaking in this manner is from my own experience and what I have seen in the lives of others in the streets. I surely do not want to come off as if I know it all, or that I have somehow attained anything. The Bible is clear on this sort of thinking.

"And why worry about a speck in your friend's eye when you have a log in your own? How can you think of saying to your friend, 'Let me help you get rid of that speck in your eye,' when you can't see past the log in your own eye? Hypocrite! First get rid of the log in your own eye; then you will see well enough to deal with the speck in your friend's eye" Matthew 7:3-5, NLT.

I realized that if I did not start looking at me, and stop looking at them: my father, my mother, my sisters, my pimp, my abusers... everyone else, but me, then I was not going to heal. It was time for change! It was time for my transformation!

Chapter 10

"Be diligent to present yourself approved to God, a worker who does not need to be ashamed, rightly dividing the word of truth."
2 Timothy 2:15, NKJV

I met Dr. Andre Sims and his wife in a parking lot in Federal Way at a barber shop. I thought it was kind of cool that they wanted to have church in a barber shop. It was real, not fake. It just felt like a place where it was safe, and we could be ourselves with no judgment and learn about Jesus. I started going to church there and I think my membership number was eleven, so there weren't many of us. I met a wonderful woman named April and her husband. I would sit in front of her because I felt safe with her. I did not feel safe around many people. I didn't feel like I was welcomed by many people in the church, but at this point, I simply did not care. I was desperate and wanted to learn more about Jesus and to walk with Him. I had already destroyed everything and everyone that meant something to me. I was baptized seven times, said the prayer of salvation many times, and went to every church denomination you can think of, with no real transformation in my life from the age of thirty-three to forty years old.

At this point, I had never learned how to walk with and gain a real relationship with Jesus Christ. Even though I call them "little prayers" that some may think meant nothing, God heard every one of them! He chose me long before I knew anything about Him. He was drawing me closer and closer to Him, but my lifestyle choices were keeping me from surrendering to His call completely. This is when I was led to Dr. Andre Sims's church. God knew what I needed and how much of it I needed, and what I was able to accept at this particular point in my life. He never forced anything on me in a way I could not handle.

God is full of love and merciful, but I had not yet experienced Him like this. I was heading on the greatest ride of my life with Jesus, and I was about to find out just how loving, graceful, and merciful He truly is. Dr. Sims invited me to church and we would have amazing Bible Studies where we would play games to learn and memorize Scripture. He also gave us a book called *The Survival Kit*, which talked about how a Christian is supposed to live and what God expects of us, biblically, from the Bible. It revealed the importance of prayer, praise, reading His Word, and serving Him and others. The first Scripture I ever learned by heart is,

"Your word I have hidden in my heart, that I might not sin against You" Psalm 119:11, NKJV.

I did not understand what any of that meant at that time. All I knew was that I needed God to hear me and that I was going to give Him my all for the first time in my entire life! I went to the altar with A LOT of problems; I was still gambling, my kids were still in disarray, I was still trying to figure out how to support my family, and every 401K I tried to build, I had to cash out to pay my rent. Life was still very chaotic, but

God began to introduce more angels into my life. The first ones were Jean and Barbara from the battered women's shelter and the homeless woman's program. The young lady from *Up & Out,* Jody Davis who took me out of prostitution. Then, God introduced me to Teresa and her mother, Jan, who helped me in so many ways to get my life in order. He was now about to introduce me to Pastor KC Cook and his wife, Zenobia and Pastor Grady Smith and his wife, Lori. These two couples were very supportive of me in the beginning and instrumental in my walk with God.

Dr. Andre Sims was an amazing preacher who knew the Word of God and I felt like I could really trust what he was saying. It was the truth! The Word of God will pierce you when it is the truth and you know it is coming from God. Even though I wasn't a Bible scholar and I was raised Catholic, the priest would actually read the Bible to us, I was not like a sponge. I loved going to the Bible Studies and learning more about Jesus. Unfortunately, a few days later, I would end up back in the casino. It was just not sticking for some reason. Each time I would go back to church, my entire soul was convicted. The guilt and the shame was overwhelming and I knew darn well it was sin for me. The Bible says what we know to be sin for us, we should not do.

"Remember, it is sin to know what you ought to do and then not do it" James 4:17, NLT.

Alcohol, drugs, compulsive overeating, gambling, prostitution, and smoking cigarettes, this was all sin for me. I couldn't just drink one glass of wine and be okay. I had stopped going to AA at this point, because Pastor Sims told me that the 12-step program was not helping or doing me any good. I was just seeking Jesus wholeheartedly to end all my issues of sin. I was twenty years sober at this time, alcohol and drugs were not my problem anymore. It was more the gambling and compulsive overeating. I listened to Pastor Sims and I did what he told me to do.

I was always getting offended. I was so broken and I was always being beaten up in some sort of way that all you had to do was look at me the wrong way, and I became offended. I had absolutely no family to back me up. Even when my daughter tried to, she eventually left and tried to start her own family due to all the toxicity she experienced in our family. Today, God is rebuilding my relationship with my daughter through her child, Nate. I am doing my best to respect her and her boundaries and be the example of what God would want me to be as a mother.

I dove into church and began going to all of the events, including the singing events. It worked for a little while and I began to stop gambling a lot and started to do better for myself. I was still very broken and needed counseling. There was no counseling available at the church so God did what He always does, He brought me an "angel". Pastor KC Cook came within about a year of us having the church, and at this point, we were meeting in an elementary school. There were women that would not let me sit beside them because I had been a prostitute; there was a lot of shaming that went on. It was the idea that I was the worst kind of sinner, but I was not going to let anyone take my "seat" from me. I was determined, at that point, that God was my last and only hope. If this wasn't going to work, I didn't know what I was going to do next.

Something in my spirit knew that this was going to work, because this was the TRUTH!

"Jesus said to him, "I am the way, the truth, and the life. No one comes to the Father except through Me" John 14:6, NKJV.

He also said that He did not come into this world to judge it, but to save it.

"For God did not send His Son into the world to condemn the world, but that the world through Him might be saved" John 3:17, NKJV.

I believed with all my heart that He was going to save me. It was surely with less than a mustard seed of faith, but I had no other choice. Pastor KC and his wife came and they were very sweet people. They came from Texas. He was a very funny man and he was always saying silly things. He had a great sense of humor. When people in the administration, or even people in the church, would say things about me, he would always stand up for me. Pastor Sims wouldn't allow it either, but he was only one person. He couldn't be there for everything, but we began what we called "Life Groups," or home groups. He would come to my home group, I guess because I was the "special needs child?"

I had two little cats and one of them jumped on top of his bald head. He did not say anything to embarrass me or make me look bad in front of the rest of the people. He just brushed that cat right off of his head and kept on moving. I will never forget that; it was extremely kind of him. I walked around most of my life with this big black X on my back; I was a "nobody," an X'd out prostitute, drug addict, gambler, and simply a loser. There was no love in my heart at all for me. When you don't have love in your own heart, it is hard for you to give love to others.

One day, Pastor KC came and I was so angry and depressed. Most of the time when I was depressed, it would come out in anger. At home, it was tears but away from home, it would turn into bitterness, binging, and all sorts of other things. I was crying and telling him about a woman that would not let me sit beside her in church. She is no longer here today, but I will not share her name. She told me that she never wanted to sit beside me and I was broken by this statement. I desperately wanted friends. I was alone for so long and I was so sad. I just wanted to belong. I just wanted to feel loved and know that I belonged somewhere.

I was completely rejected, even in the Church. I did not even know how to take this. Pastor KC told me to read this scripture, and it has stuck with me since that day:

"For I know the thoughts that I think toward you, says the Lord, thoughts of peace and not of evil, to give you a future and a hope. Then you will call upon Me and go and pray to Me, and I will listen to you. And you will seek Me and find Me, when you search for Me with all your heart" Jeremiah 29:11-13, NKJV.

This scripture began to give me some sort of peace in my life, a glimmer of hope that maybe I wasn't going to be homeless or live in a mobile home when I was sixty years old. Maybe, my kids were going to have a normal life at some point. Maybe, everything that I wanted for my family would come true. I kept going in my walk with God and I was working at Food Services of America trying not to gamble, but I fell short a few times. Then, 9/11 happened and I lost my job. I got another job at a company called OnVia.com and I was making pretty good money. Not poverty level, but where I was able to live a little better. My anxiety was getting worse and you could tell things were not good. My chemistry began to change because I was entering perimenopause, and I did not know what that was going to look like for me.

Pastor KC really encouraged me during this season of my life and then God introduced me to a woman named Julia, angel number six. This woman has never made a fake statement in the twenty-two years that I have known her. Her and her husband are both very real people and love God, and they love to help others. Julia took me under her wings, and so did Earl in some ways, but mostly Julia. Her and her cousin A.D. would come over, and I loved him so very much. He was disabled and older. I would help to take care of him while they were away and he would come and help me clean my house. I would go and have dinner with them and ask my questions from the study the night before, asking what Pastor Sims meant by this, or other questions I needed answers to, and they would answer them for me. Julia is, to this day, one of my most special friends. I will forever love the truth in her and how willing she was to share it with a sinner like me.

I began to paint scriptures to memorize them, and me and my daughter would go to this ceramic store to get items to paint my scriptures on. One particular scripture is Ephesians 3:17-20, which says,

"Then Christ will make his home in your hearts as you trust in him. Your roots will grow down into God's love and keep you strong. And may you have the power to understand, as all God's people should, how wide, how long, how high, and how deep his love is. May you experience the love of Christ, though it is too great to understand fully. Then you will be made complete with all the fullness of life and power that comes from God. Now all glory to God, who is able, through his mighty power

at work within us, to accomplish infinitely more than we might ask or think," NLT.

I began to learn more about the Book of Ephesians in church and how much God loved us. The first chapter of Ephesians tells you all about who you are in Christ. So, if you were adopted in the world, or thrown away like I was, whatever your hurt is or whatever your angst is, the Good News is that God says we are all adopted into the Kingdom of Heaven. It goes on to say that we are given every spiritual blessing from above through Christ Jesus. Everything God has, we get too. He has given us all of these gifts, and He has also given us the Holy Spirit as the vehicle to walk in these gifts every single day of our lives. But if we are not living in the Spirit, or walking in the Spirit, we are never going to learn to achieve these things in our lives. God does not force us, or take our free will away from us.

Julia and I would go swimming and we would hang out together. She ended up discipling me, along with Pastor KC and Lori and Grady, at this point. She would come and help me clean my house. I have been obese most of my life and I was working full time with my kids participating in sports, so it was very hard for me to get all that I needed done in my position. She was a true angel, and she would bring her son, Jeremiah. He was about three or four years old, and I would bring him Teriyaki. He liked it so much. He was such a sweet little boy.

When my son shot the twelve year old, they came over to my house every day to help me. I was so depressed that my son was in prison. Every traumatic experience that happened in my life, they came out and ministered to me. Pastor Sims was a solo pastor of a very large church at that time; it was hard for him to take the time to minister personally to his congregants. I don't judge him for this at all, he was very good to me. I was just looking for someone to protect me, as I had never been protected. I just wanted a family, someone to just accept me and my children as their family.

I continued to hang out with Julia, go to church, and I served in the Outreach Ministry. I found that in my depression, serving was truly the best thing for me. It would help to take my mind off of all of the things that were going on in my life. At this time, God brought angel number nine into my life, Elder Stephen McNeal and his wife Bonnie. They had come to our church from Iowa, I believe, with six beautiful babies. In the year of 2000, I began helping children at Christmas. I had decided that because God had always helped my children when we were poor, that I was going to give back. I found a vehicle through a lady named Linda who had a non-profit organization in a church called the *Light of Christ* in Federal Way, Washington. They helped me with purchasing gift cards, other gifts, and would help me to give out the gifts on the streets. It was a wonderful beginning to a very long-lasting ministry.

Elder Stephen McNeal looked at me one day when I was down and out, and said to me, "You are the Luke 7:47 Woman." I didn't even know what that meant, so I went to look it up:

"Then one of the Pharisees asked Him to eat with him. And He went to the Pharisee's house, and sat down to eat. And behold, a woman in the city who was a sinner, when she knew that Jesus sat at the table in the Pharisee's house, brought an alabaster flask of fragrant oil, and stood at His feet behind Him weeping; and she began to wash His feet with her tears, and wiped them with the hair of her head; and she kissed His feet and anointed them with the fragrant oil. Now when the Pharisee

who had invited Him saw this, he spoke to himself, saying, "This Man, if He were a prophet, would know who and what manner of woman this is who is touching Him, for she is a sinner."

"And Jesus answered and said to him, "Simon, I have something to say to you." So he said, "Teacher, say it." "There was a certain creditor who had two debtors. One owed five hundred denarii, and the other fifty. And when they had nothing with which to repay, he freely forgave them both. Tell Me, therefore, which of them will love him more?" Simon answered and said, "I suppose the one whom he forgave more."

"And He said to him, "You have rightly judged." Then He turned to the woman and said to Simon, "Do you see this woman? I entered your house; you gave Me no water for My feet, but she has washed My feet with her tears and wiped them with the hair of her head. You gave Me no kiss, but this woman has not ceased to kiss My feet since the time I came in. You did not anoint My head with oil, but this woman has anointed My feet with fragrant oil. **Therefore I say to you, her sins, which are many, are forgiven, for she loved much. But to whom little is forgiven, the same loves little.**"

"Then He said to her, "Your sins are forgiven." And those who sat at the table with Him began to say to themselves, "Who is this who even forgives sins?" Then He said to the woman, "Your faith has saved you. Go in peace" Luke 7:36-50, NKJV (emphasis).

The scripture is speaking of a woman, a sinner, and everyone is asking, "Why is she here? Why would you invite her?" This is what legalism is all about. These were supposedly "Christian" people asking why this woman was at their dinner. Was she not good enough? I felt like this more times than I can count in many churches I attended. I feel like they put a label on me that I wasn't "good enough" to be in their church. As Christians, we do not have the right to judge anyone who chooses to be gay, is a drug or alcohol addict, a prostitute, a gambler, a sex offender, someone that has gone to prison, or any other sin for that matter. God is the only judge! He is the only one that has the right to judge sin in that arena. If someone comes to your church begging to repent, and turning away from their sin, you are supposed to receive them and restore them. You are to correct that person in love, not reject them.

"Dear brothers and sisters, if another believer is overcome by some sin, you who are godly should gently and humbly help that person back onto the right path. And be careful not to fall into the same temptation yourself" Galatians 6:1, NLT.

We are supposed to help them see that the wages of sin is death. We are supposed to help them see that we all have sinned and fallen short of the glory of God. That it is a free gift. We do not have to work for God's love. We are to let them know that if they confess with their mouth that Jesus is Lord and that God raised Him from the dead, they shall be saved (Romans 10:9-10).

God has brought all these angels into my life, a very broken, angry, anxious, and afraid soul. I am so grateful and thankful for every one of them who counted it not robbery to sow seeds of love, prayers, and support for me and my family.

My daughter was finally going to Youth Camp at this time, and my oldest son was in prison. My youngest son was extremely mad at me for giving him up for adoption and no amount of explanation or apology was going to change his mind about me, at that time. He was in Kansas and it was very difficult to form a relationship with him. One day, I was in the casino and my anxiety was kicking in real heavy. My face was turning red and my entire body was overheated. I was losing thousands of dollars that I did not have. My mother helped to enable me by giving me money, but I was very manipulative and broken still trying to hold on to this one area of my life even though I knew it was sin. I knew it was unpleasing to God.

I desperately needed to stop trying to fix my own depression and worrying about what others thought about me. I was punishing myself with gambling. It was no longer fun. I remember coming home one night after losing all my money, and there was no food in the refrigerator to feed my kids. I had saved twenty bucks just so I could take them to Burger King to get a .99 hamburger, praying I would find money somewhere. Gambling was a vicious end to a vicious cycle I had lived in all my life.

There is Good News… yes, the good news is that it was all dying inside of me through the healing power and love of Jesus Christ! He was slowly, but surely, convicting me and healing me to move away from that lifestyle.

Elyse's Youth Leader, April Lee, was a sweet woman of God. She would now be my tenth angel God sent into my life. She would come to my house and cut my hair because I really did struggle with going places. I had severe anxiety disorder and struggled with traveling in a vehicle. She was a gentle soul with a kind heart. One day, I was at the casino, and my daughter had had more than enough of me, so she called

April and asked her if she could go and get me out of the casino. I had $1500 bucks in front of me on the PiaGow table and I was finally winning for the first time in a while. April walks in and I say, "Oh, hey April, what's going on?" It occurred to me that she was walking into a casino, and not a church. She said, "Well, we're going to cash out today." I said, "Oh, okay?" I was embarrassed as I could not get help, and mad at Elyse for exposing my sin to everyone, and that she was enjoying it. But Elyse was a teenager and needed a mother. I was not being much of a mother.

April talked to me on the way home and she said, "Susan, I know it is tough, but you have a daughter at home who needs you." She then said, "I know you are struggling but you need to find a way to stop doing this." I knew she was right but every time I would find a way to get away from it, I just could not find a good reason not to go back. Something would always trigger me, and I would go back to gambling. I really tried to help others and do good for other people, so I would stop gambling. I began to do Outreach, as well, but it was just not enough. I still didn't really trust God, and I was still stuck in my trauma.

My son Eric was angry and hurt and when he came to visit from Kansas, it wasn't the reunion visits I had dreamed of, nor was he willing to forgive me. He simply kept me in his life for a means to an end. It broke me inside, but I knew I loved him, so I continued to allow this behavior. I didn't cope well with Eric's rejection, and I made my way to the casino to drown in my shame and sorrows. When I got back, I was angry because I had lost all our money. Elyse and Eric were sitting at the table, and I began fighting with Elyse about something and Eric jumped in to stop the fight. Elyse was tired of my gambling habit and our life. I used to call her expectation *the Channel 39 family* (Disney) but in all rights, she was a child and deserved a life of functionality, love, and peace. Something I was only able to do in a short order at this point in my life. Elyse deserved that, just like Elliot did, and just like Eric. Unfortunately, I was never going to be the kind of parent that could offer that to them. I was already too far gone. She was around thirteen or fourteen by this time.

Elyse was so smart and intelligent. I would always encourage her to spend time around healthy families, like Terry Idler, her friend Darcy's mom and dad. There was also Denise Pac, these were my angels who helped me to raise my child. They helped to get her to her soccer tournaments when I could not drive or when there was too much drama going on, she could spend the night with their families. They helped her have somewhat of a normal childhood, and I am very grateful and thankful to both of them for helping me during a very devastating time in my life.

Eric went home at this point, and a few months later, I get a call from his girlfriend Sweetpea. Eric had called me at one point and told me that he had gotten shot in his ankle. I was always trying to find out where he was and how he was doing, even from far away. There was a joke going around that his mother was all over Facebook trying to find out where he was. I was a very good private investigator. I couldn't physically get on a plane from Seattle and go and take care of him. Thank God for Jerry and Teresa, his adoptive parents. There were some things that were not very good between us, but most of it was because of my own shame and inability to do my job as a parent. I am so very grateful to them for how they raised him and the life that they gave him. I am eternally grateful for all they have done for my son. I also say this to my daughter and other son's families; you all took very good care of my kids when I could not.

Eric was running hard at this point. He was seventeen years old and living a gang banger life, and I was scared to death. My son Elliot had just come out of that life and was in prison, so I did not want this for Eric's life. Eric called me and was very depressed. I could not figure out what was wrong with him, so I spoke with his girlfriend and she tells me he is not in a good place emotionally. Next thing I hear is a phone call telling me that Eric has been shot by the police and they were rushing him to the ER and into surgery. I called my pastor but he was too busy to come over and help me. Two women from my biblical counseling class, Jane and Sue, came over to sit with me. They sat with me and prayed with me, and I was just devastated. I called my mom as well and just could not get myself together. This was an extremely dark time for me. I was beginning to develop a relationship with God, so I was able to ask Him to help me. I had some knowledge of Scripture at this point, so I could speak them over my life and it helped a little. I was still in deep pain. I sat there and cried profusely. My greatest fear was that this exact thing was going to happen to Eric, and that it was all my fault.

The guilt, the shame, and the remorse I was carrying was overwhelming and unbelievable. I was frantically calling all around to talk to the police and many other people. I found out that he was shot once in the stomach and they did not know he was shot again, until after the surgery was over and he was still bleeding. He had been shot in the back and he was now paralyzed. The bullet was lodged in his spine, and they were sure he would be paralyzed. I was devastated! I could not get the thoughts out of my head that this was all my fault, because I was not the kind of mother he needed as a child. I sat in that tiny apartment with nothing, with no one, and truly nowhere in my right mind, praying and asking God to help him and to help me, as well.

I finally got a call that he was going to live and that he was being released. The paralysis was in his lower leg and he would have to get a brace for his leg to walk. He would have to go to physical therapy for a while, but that was welcomed news knowing that he was okay and going to live. What had actually happened that day was that my son had called the police on himself. I think they called it "suicide by police," or at least that is what some call it. They shot at my son thirty-four times. My son did not have a gun on him, only a cell phone. I can understand the first shot not knowing that he was holding a phone, instead of a gun, but he was wearing a cast on his foot from being shot two weeks earlier. He came out holding his cell phone up and they shot him once in the stomach. He fell to the ground and his cell phone fell away from him. They proceeded to shoot thirty-four more bullets at a seventeen year old child.

Sadly, we know what took place on this day. The police tried to kill my African American son in Wichita, Kansas. I was angry and began calling all around to lawyers, the prosecutor, and many others trying to get justice for my son. Well, the Wichita police began covering their tracks and stating they had witnesses and even wrote an article in the newspaper about how police officers have PTSD (Post Traumatic Stress Disorder) in these "volatile" situations. Listen, I know we are commanded to forgive people, and this has been a really hard one for me. Regardless, God really used this for His glory in the end. If I don't forgive you, God cannot forgive me, or vice versa according to the Word of God.

"But if you refuse to forgive others, your Father will not forgive your sins" Matthew 6:15, NLT.

I had to forgive the Kansas State Police officers for trying to kill my son, and they charged him with deadly assault against a police officer when he did not have a weapon whatsoever, only his cell phone. Instead of sending my son to a mental hospital for suicidal tendencies, he was sent to prison for four years. He is now considered a "violent offender" who was convicted of trying to "kill" police officers. I am extremely terrified that the next time they see him, they may very well indeed kill my son. This was a very traumatic season in my life, and in our family.

My past, and I believe even my children's fathers' past, was now catching up with us and trickling down into our children's lives. Something had to change, and change fast for our family.

Chapter 11

Praise Him in the Storm

"The Lord is my strength and song, And He has become my salvation; He is my God, and I will praise Him; My father's God, and I will exalt Him." Exodus 15:2, NKJV

One thing I was learning in my Christian walk, at this point, was that even though there was still a lot of depression, anxiety, and off and on gambling going on, I was learning, growing, and trusting God a little bit more every day. My pastor, Dr. Sims, was a preaching machine; he taught the Word of God with power and with clarity. The first scripture I learned with our Survival Kit Bible study was, *"I have hidden your word in my heart that I might not sin against thee"* Psalms 119:11. I was growing so much, and I also had Pastor KC Cook, Elder Steph, and Julia who were mentoring me. Pastor KC was real and honest. He would tell me the truth when I was thinking wrong, but he did it in a way that was gentle, funny, and full of love. His wife Zenobia is a true, pure woman of God. She was kind to me and would let me babysit her children. One night, I had fallen asleep on their couch and she put a blanket on me. This was the kindest thing anyone had done for me in twenty years. Elder Stephen really began to help me walk through a lot of my dark times.

I began to delve into helping the homeless. This is when God brought another angel into my life, sweet Roberta. She helped me to start a homeless meal outreach at her church Bible Fellowship on the way home from my church, *Christ the King Bible Fellowship*. We started the meals on Monday and then the *Dream Center* came into play. They helped to take sack lunches, hygiene items, and all kinds of donated items to people in motels, out in the streets, and in the forests. I took over the motels in that area, there were four of them. I would go out every day to help, and during the week nights, I would go and check on the kids to make sure they were getting in the bed and that their mother's weren't getting high around them. I would try to help encourage the mothers and I would also go out into the streets and share the Gospel with prostitutes and addicts. This is where I just gave my life to Christ through ministry.

I began to feel so much better as I was serving in the streets. When depression tried to hit me, ministering in the streets brought me great joy. It still does to this day, twenty odd years later. I still have great joy when ministering to God's people.

"So he answered and said, "'You shall love the Lord your God with all your heart, with all your soul, with all your strength, and with all your mind,' and 'your neighbor as yourself'" Luke 10:27, NKJV.

My husband always preaches when it comes to this Scripture that you must first learn to love yourself. At this particular time, I was still not in a position where I could honestly love myself, or felt any self-love towards me. I was a little bit less judgmental of myself, but not much. My mother helped me to open up a coffee stand with my inheritance, this would be business number two that was going to help me and my kids out of our financial situation. My mother tried to help, and I tried to do better but unfortunately, I was still not in a good place and this hindered me from prospering and receiving the blessing of God in my life. The gambling became much worse and I put all of my money into this business, not knowing that the city was about to remodel Pacific Highway and shut down the entire coffee stand. Here she is, my mother, who invested my inheritance while she was alive, only to lose it all. Here I was once again in the middle of a mess trying to figure out what I was going to do.

I tried to recover it by delivering coffee. I would deliver all over the city to homes and businesses to keep it going. It was just not working. I could not hire anyone because I could not afford it. The debts were getting higher and the money was getting lower. I started gambling again trying to get the money back, truly a stupid idea for anyone. The casino always wins! Even if you are just going to have fun, and I never had fun at the casino; the casino is the only one that ends up winning. They are run by the mob so good luck having anyone that is going to be nice to you there. I had finally made the decision to stop gambling and began going to a support group through a Bible study. I tried to make amends with my mother. I sold the coffee stand and gave her back whatever money I received from the sale because I wanted to show her I was different. I paid off all the debts so she wouldn't have to. Unfortunately, I believe she did not want to tell my other family members the truth that she gave me my inheritance, but I know my mother loved me and my children. The coffee shop was a total loss, so I had no idea what I was going to do next.

I then found out she was dying of cancer. She was my only family left and I was devastated. Once again, the guilt and remorse of what a nasty human being I was is stuck in my mind and my heart, and I had to finally face it. I would send my mother scriptures every day so she could put them up around her to encourage her. She would call me and say, "Am I going to Heaven?" I would tell her, "Mama, you got saved as a Protestant on April 7, 1941, and you've been a Catholic for over fifty years. You're going to Heaven." I asked her if she believed that Jesus Christ was the Son of God and that He died and rose on the third day and that He is seated at the right hand of the Father, and she said, "Of course I do, Susie." I said to her, "Mama, did you accept Him into your life and ask Him to forgive you?" She said, "Yes, I did." I said to her, "Well, then you are going to Heaven."

I may not have had anything else that I have done right in my entire life, but I got to share the Gospel with my mother at a time when she was terrified. Romans 3:23 (NKJV) says, *"... for all have sinned and fall short of the glory of God,"* and Romans 4:4-5 (NLT) says, *"When people work, their wages are not a gift, but something they have earned. But people are counted as righteous, not because of their work, but because of their faith in God who forgives sinners."* (The Promise) Romans 10:9-10 says: *"If you declare with your mouth, "Jesus is Lord," and believe in your heart that God raised him from the dead, you will be saved. For it is with your heart that you believe and are justified, and it is with your mouth that you profess your faith and are saved."*

My mother also had a spirit of fear and anxiety that followed her, her entire life. My mom was scared and my sisters were tirelessly taking care of her. She did have family with her in the latter years of her life who took really good care of her. All of which had families and kids themselves, but they still made their way to help their mother. I am really proud of my sisters for taking care of my mom. I took care of her in the only way I knew, which was to share the Gospel and share scriptures to encourage her in her last days. My mother died on April 6, 2006, and my son, Elliot, was just out of prison so he was able to attend his grandmother's funeral. He loved her so much. Elyse was in New York with her class, so she was not able to go to the funeral. My friends Julia and Earl paid for my way to go down there because I was not able to, but it was still very hard for me because my anxiety while traveling was very great.

I went down to Portland to bury my mother and my sisters were not very happy with me, understandably. I was not living a good life for a very long time. I was living with shame, guilt, and remorse which did not end up well. I went to my mother's funeral and one of my sisters did not want me there, while one of my other sisters held my hand to help me get into the funeral. I walked in with them as a family, but at the reception afterwards, I was not welcomed at the family table. At this point, I was probably at the lowest point of my life. I was trying to let God redeem me; I was really trying to change. I had finally let go of the gambling and doing my best to let it all go. I really wanted to walk right with God, but I realized that the people around me were not going to be happy for me, because I had burned too many bridges. It is easy to expect people to simply love and forgive you, and move on, but it is not that simple. Only a mature Christian can truly forgive like this. I did not blame anyone at that point for not wanting me in their lives. I didn't even want to be there; I was still a pretty miserable human being.

After my mother's death, I began seeing a biblical counselor from *Christ the King Fellowship* named Chuck. I also began to see pastors at my Pastor's sister's church facility. I was trying really hard to stay on track. The agoraphobia was getting really bad and my world was getting very small. I couldn't go to the back of the grocery store without having a panic attack. My functioning skills were becoming worse by the day.

My friend Julia became the best gift God could have given me at this time in my life. She befriended me by inviting me to her home for long talks and very tasty meals. We would go swimming at LA Fitness and talk for hours. Julia's biblical knowledge is wide and great, and she would pour into my life. I was so broken and depressed and bitter. Julia would speak the truth of God's Word into my life even when it hurt really bad. I began to really look at myself and not all the people who lived in my head condemned me. Revelations 12:10 says, *"Then I heard a loud voice in heaven say: "Now have come the salvation and the power and the kingdom of our God, and the authority of his Messiah. For the accuser of our brothers and sisters, who accuses them before our God day and night, has been hurled down."*

When Elyse was about sixteen or seventeen, she was pretty much done with me and my depression and anxiety. She met her boyfriend of many years now, and she moved out of my home. I was now all alone. I didn't have my mother, my last bit of family. I didn't have my daughter. My son had gotten married after he got out of prison and was living with his wife. My other son in Kansas really hated me and was doing his own thing at that point. I had no family, nothing! It was me, myself, and pitiful I. I was at the lowest I had ever been in my life, but I wasn't going to give up on God. I knew that God was my only hope. I knew that if I continued to serve Him, that I could find some joy in that area. I really started to serve God wholeheartedly. I began to serve meals to the homeless and helping prostitutes on the streets with Roberta for many years. I just started to throw myself into service. The downfall of my lack of faith in God was the fact that I used food for every emotion I had instead of renewing my mind with God's Word, the true food for life. The result of this was obesity, which has affected my entire life.

I was looking for a job in Federal Way and found one that was looking for a bill collector. I started working but I hated working in an office due to my severe anxiety. I did not like the elevators because I am very claustrophobic. I was obese at this point, I was growing larger and larger by the day. It was very hard for me to physically function. I told the employer that I needed to quit because it was just too much for me. He asked me if I could work from home, would I stay and work for him. I agreed! I worked from home when working from home was not a thing. When I worked at this particular job, I had this continual felony looming over my head for promoting prostitution.

When they wanted me to sign paperwork to initiate a background check on me, my heart dropped to my stomach! I just knew they were going to fire me. I ran into the owner's office and began to tell him my story. He was such a kind, compassionate, and strong man that listened to me tell him all about my past. He looked at me and said, "Well, are you still doing this?" I was forty two years old and 350 plus pounds at this time. I told him no and explained that I had not lived in that lifestyle since 1995. I had been out of prostitution for about eleven years. He said, "Okay, well we do not have to talk about this anymore and I am going to hire you." He told me he saw talent in me that he needed to help him in this business. This was about seventeen years ago. Along with an amazing group of other employees, I helped this man go from four attorneys to around forty attorneys to this day. I still, to this day, collect about 98% of his revenue before they bill it. God knew that day that He had a plan for my life and that every month like clockwork when month end hits, I ask GOD to collect that money and every month God comes through for me and shows me favor. Although, the owner of this firm and his wonderfully talented wife are my favorite people, I know that GOD is the One who provided for me when I couldn't provide for myself.

This was God's financial plan for my life. I am eternally grateful to Him for this employment and the people I work for, because of the favor HE has given me for the last eighteen years. When we go to work, our true employer is Jesus. As long as you serve HIM first, HE will never let you down. God places favor upon His kids. When you walk in His will, His perfect and loving will, He will bless you abundantly and answer your prayers. Even if you are not walking fully in His will, He can still show you unmerited favor for whatever reason He decides. I was a convicted felon. There should be no natural way for me to have received this job, let alone to be blessed in the many ways God has blessed and favored me.

"For I know the thoughts that I think toward you, says the Lord, thoughts of peace and not of evil, to give you a future and a hope. Then you will call upon Me and go and pray to Me, and I will listen to you. And you will seek Me and find Me, when you search for Me with all your heart" Jeremiah 29:11-13, NKJV.

Though I was blessed with an amazing job and being taken care of financially, I still did not have any kids with me. I was chasing down my youngest son trying to get him to forgive me, telling him how much I loved him and how much I needed him back in my life. I had been doing this for years, even though it was the wrong way to go about it, but it was all I knew how to do. He did not want to hear anything I had to say, and rejected me. I threw myself back into ministry.

One day, I was back out on the streets sharing the Gospel of Jesus Christ, it was a Sunday, and I was at the grocery outlet. There were four girls working the stroll and I ran over to minister to them; two of them got into cars with tricks, one went the other way, and I was left with one girl. She was a beautiful African American and Caucasian girl with blue/green eyes. She was absolutely breathtaking. I could smell the alcohol on her and it looked like she was nodding off heroin. I am not sure, but she was definitely high. I looked at her and I said, "Sweetheart, there are men out here that want to kill you and I want to help you. Will you let me help you get into treatment today?" I began to minister to her and she gave me a big hug, because it seemed she really needed it. She told me she knew all about men that wanted to kill her. I asked her how and she turned around and the name "Kelly" was tattooed on her. I asked her, "Honey, who is Kelly?" She said to me, "Kelly McGinnis was my mother. She was the fourth victim of the Green River Killer."

I just stood there stunned with tears rolling down my face. I said to her, "Sweetheart, I met your mama when I was eighteen years old. When I went to jail for the first time as a prostitute, your mom held my hand all weekend in the jail cell." I proceeded to tell her, "When I went back two weeks later, they told me that she had been murdered." I told her that her mama would want her to go and get treatment. That little girl had no idea what was happening in that moment, but the power and love of Jesus Christ fell all over me. God showed me that His power and love was going to reign and He allowed me to see His glory in a full circle by leading me directly to Kelly's daughter. I met a young lady that helped me through a prison cell some thirty odd years earlier and then, He let me meet her daughter.

Do you know that God is so big??? Don't you ever limit what He can do in your life! As I was coming out of my own trauma, losing my entire family, and ending my gambling addiction, He was using me to help someone else out of their trauma. Him taking my family away was probably the best thing that could have happened to me at that time, as it caused me to shift my thinking. When I was around my family, all that exuded from me was guilt, shame, remorse, anxiety, and depression. I was not good for them in that state. The enemy would bring up my past and all that I had endured so often that it affected me greatly. The devil is the accuser of the brethren. He will accuse you night and day! But God says something different about you, about me.

"This means that anyone who belongs to Christ has become a new person. The old life is gone; a new life has begun!" 2 Corinthians 5:17, NLT.

I was a new creation in Christ, but how was I going to be able to convince my children who had been traumatized by my lifestyle that I had changed? They could not stand me. They thought I was a loser, a gambler, and not any kind of loving mother. My own trauma caused much of what I experienced in my life, but at some point, we all will have to look in that mirror and stop blaming everyone else. We have to come to terms that we all have a real enemy that desires to destroy our lives and to take a stand and refuse to allow him any more room to do so. We need to begin to follow the precepts and the laws of love in Christ Jesus. He is truly the Way, the Truth, and the Life. He will transform your life into something you could have never imagined!

I was beginning to have a little bit of hope. The gambling was gone and I didn't have the shame every day along with that vicious cycle. I was left in great debt, but God had given me a great job and I was able to work from home, so that I could do ministry part time. It was wonderful. For me, it was a win/win situation and it was probably the happiest time of my entire life. I was still without my family and still struggled with deep seated emotions, but I could truly see myself serving God for the rest of my life. That was the least I could do for all He had brought me through during my life. He pulled me out of that deep, dark pit that I had put myself in, and He was pulling me out more and more every day. This is called *sanctification*. It is the process of being set apart for God's purposes, but it is not an overnight thing. We are all being sanctified daily and will continue to be sanctified until we meet our Lord.

"Then Christ will make his home in your hearts as you trust in him. Your roots will grow down into God's love and keep you strong. And may you have the power to understand, as all God's people should, how wide, how long, how high, and how deep his love is. May you experience the love of Christ, though it is too great to understand fully. Then you will be made complete with all the fullness of life and power that comes from God. Now all glory to God, who is able, through his mighty power at work within us, to accomplish infinitely more than we might ask or think" Ephesians 3:17-20, NLT.

Pastor Sims used to say, "Some of us come to the altar with carry-on bags. Some come with a couple of bags of luggage. Some of us have to pull our luggage in a cart. And some of us bring an entire train of bags behind us that we are dragging from our past." Well, that was me. I knew I was the worst of the worst, in my eyes. I still had Julia in my life

147

and the many other "angels" that God had sent into my life to help me walk through those very dark and lonely times.

I began to continue to build the ministry God had given me. I wrote the vision down and sent it to Pastor Sims and my elder, Stephen, for approval. It was called *The Alabaster Ministry* and the ministry was beginning on the streets where I came from and sharing the Gospel. It was moving into discipleship housing and a big program to help women to heal from the effects of prostitution, addiction, homelessness, depression, and anxiety. All the things I was suffering with myself. I was getting better, but I did not have one of those "Oh God has healed me of everything moments" overnight. But when Christ entered my life, when Holy Spirit came to live within me, I was eternally healed. I was going to eternally live with God. I knew I was going to have that "blink of an eye" experience and meet Him in Heaven. I truly believed this truth. God kept blessing me here and there and putting people into my life that weren't family, but loved me as if I was family. They saw good things within me, even when I did not.

I had all kinds of counseling off and on, like Chuck, the biblical counselor, that was helping me. I had another lady from *Hope Place* that counseled me. I always had some kind of counseling going on, but it was like I was waiting for this "Aha" moment where everything would be perfect. Unfortunately, it never happened. This is what sanctification is all about. It was in God's timing and in God's perfect will for my life. Yet, I kept on moving doing Bible studies and learning more from mature women of God. I was hungry for the Word of God.

"Blessed are those who hunger and thirst for righteousness, For they shall be filled" Matthew 5:6, NKJV.

148

I have never been a great Bible reader. I am not going to lie and tell anyone that because my husband knows me and will tell everyone that is not the truth. I have a very hard time sitting still and doing anything for very long. If I am not doing sixteen tasks at one time, I am not happy. I love to listen to God's Word whether I am at church, watching it on my phone, or delving into Bible studies with others, but to sit down and read the Bible cover to cover, I never have and I'm not sure if I ever will. Some may be able to, but for me, at this point, it is just not how I receive or retain His Word. It is definitely a goal that I am working on with the Lord. However you are better able to receive, let that be personal to you; between you and God. We are all walking daily to grow closer and closer to Him, don't beat yourself up if you are not where someone else "may be," or you think they may be. Do the best you can with what you have and He will do the rest.

I finally met another "angel" in my life named Pastor Roy. Pastor Roy was my leader over the *Dream Center* as I ministered in that program. What a man of God he was, gentle, kind, and just real. He loved God and there was no judgment in his heart. He was just one of those people you couldn't razzle easily. He was on his focus for the Lord, and that is where he stayed. I truly enjoyed what we were doing for the women in the streets. One night, there was a woman that was having DT's and struggling with her addiction. One woman took her twelve year old son so he would be safe, while the emergency responders helped her. I did not do these things for any glory or for others to see what I was doing. I did it because I loved to help people, as so many had helped me in my darkest times. God says to do things in secret.

"Watch out! Don't do your good deeds publicly, to be admired by others, for you will lose the reward from your Father in heaven. When you give to someone in need, don't do as the hypocrites do—blowing trumpets in the synagogues and streets to call attention to their acts of charity! I tell you the truth, they have received all the reward they will ever get. But when you give to someone in need, don't let your left hand know what your right hand is doing. Give your gifts in private, and your Father, who sees everything, will reward you" Matthew 6:1-4, NLT.

I knew who the glory belonged to and I was not going to take that glory from Him. I knew that the King of kings and the Lord of lords was my only hope. My best efforts got me to 2nd and Pike, pregnant with no shoes, socks, coat, or bra standing on the street corner in the middle of a snowstorm turning a forty dollar trick. My righteousness is as the Bible says, "… as *filthy rags*." But I was on the boat now, I was clinging for dear life with God. I got on that water and I was walking with Jesus. I was scared to death, but I knew if I took my eyes off of Him, I would drown.

A friend of mine named Cathy introduced me to another program where they helped drug addicts and where they would have a meal and have Bible study called *Bible Fellowship*. I gathered a bunch of homeless folks together and took them there to get a meal. I was desperately trying to feel better in a lot of ways by doing this kind of work. I knew I couldn't work for God's love, which had been clearly ingrained in my head by Pastor Sims. I did know that the power of God was all over me when I served Him. So, was I selfishly looking for that *feeling* when I served Him? Probably, due to my depression, anxiety, and fear, and how broken I was. I just wanted to continue to do what God was calling me to do and not revert back to my old lifestyle.

From the Green River to the Lily of the Valley

I went to the *Bible Fellowship* one day, and there was this really handsome man standing there with a ladder to get a sign put up. He had on what we called a "zuit suit" similar to what Pastor Sims used to wear, and he turned around and looked at me. I thought to myself that this man would never be interested in a woman like me. Then, as I was getting out of my car, one of the ladies said, "Ms. Susan!" I said, "What?" She looked at me and said to me that she heard me make a noise as if this man was really handsome. I kept walking and he followed me in the door. I turned around and told him that I didn't have any money, so if that is what he was looking for, then he needed to turn around. I had such a bitter demeanor especially when it came to men. I did not trust anyone and had a terrible attitude towards everyone.

This man did not give up and followed me all over that place. I gave him my church card and told him if he was interested in me, then he needed to call my pastor. I was not going to go backwards again. I had not, at this point, been with a man in thirteen years. I had chosen celibacy. He eventually called Pastor Sims and reached out to me, and he wanted to come and join us in feeding the homeless. The next time I went to church, he was there and he walked up to me with a picture of a woman. I asked him who it was and he said it was his wife. He proceeded to tell me that she died while he was in prison. She looked almost just like me, same size, same color of hair; it was strange, as we looked like we could be twins. My heart broke for him, this was really sad to hear about what happened to his wife while he was in treatment.

We had a Valentine's event at our church, and I bought a beautiful dress. A sister at the church took a picture of both of us in our dresses. She was a lawyer and since I worked for a law firm, I really clung to her and we hit it off well. I really thought I was going to meet someone that night as something in my spirit kept telling me that God was going to bring the right man into my life. I did not meet him that night, but I continued serving, working, and living my life the best way I knew how. I was at peace even though it was pretty lonely.

Eventually, I began to see Toney, off and on, the man that I thought was really handsome. We began to do ministry together and it was apparent that I was completely smitten with him. Unfortunately, we did exactly what I promised God I would not do, until I was married again. We fornicated and I lost my job. I thought that God must be punishing me because of my sin. It turns out, He had a different plans for me. I moved into the Women's home where Toney was ministering. I was assisting the leader of the home with many things as I had come out of so much, but I did not realize how sick I still was from my past: emotionally, mentally, and spiritually. Going to church and sitting underneath the teaching of Pastor Sims was like a six-course steak dinner; I had never been under a teaching like his ever in my life. I grew so much during that time; I was a born-again believer at this point for almost five years. I was still a "baby in Christ," if you will, but I hungered and thirst for the Word of God, and I was being filled not only at my church, but by my friend Julia who was also pouring into my life even when I did not like what she had to say. I sometimes would get offended and leave, but I always came back and she welcomed me with open arms.

So, here I was in the Women's house and Toney was in the Men's house, which cut down on the fornication for us, praise God! He was in his own treatment plan and was not supposed to be seeing me. I didn't know that until I was already in love with him. Everyone knew we liked each other, but we couldn't really see each other that much as I was in the Women's house. I was so very excited because I had always wanted to help women. I met a wonderful woman, another one of my "angels" at the home, her name is Cricket. Funny, I met her as she was fighting with another woman over a lighter. I was the leader in the house that weekend, so I had to figure out what to do. I called the pastor over and he came in and broke up the fight and settled everyone down. This is how it was in the discipleship houses, women would fight and steal from one another. This was normal.

Soon, Christmas time came around and I began the Toy program but this time in the Women's house where there were children. I decorated the place beautifully and bought all of the women gifts and distributed toys to the children. Again, I always wanted to give back as so many helped me and my children when I was struggling in the streets myself. I knew what it felt like to be a single mom with nothing at Christmas and many other times. I have helped women and men at Christmas for over twenty-five years now and we are registered with Toys for Tots now. What a joy this has been in my recovery. I began to get to know the women a lot more and really had to get real with myself and real with them. Toney and I were not supposed to be seeing each other, so I had to cut it off with him because things were just not adding up and there was just not peace or trust between us. I had to confess before the women in the house and ask for their forgiveness because I was supposed to be an example to them. Well, that began to happen after I cut it off with Toney. I told them that if God wanted us together after we left the houses, then He would have to do that, but as of this point, I wanted to truly witness to these women how to do it the right way.

Friends of mine, Jane and Sue, had a Bible study called *By the Hem of His Garment*, which targeted how to heal from abortion but overall, how to heal from so many things. I thought it would be a really good thing for the women in the home, but boy did I really begin to receive some much needed healing in my own life. *Bible Fellowship* did believe in the gifts of the Spirit, so they had people to come and prophesy to the women at the house. Pastor Bob's pastor had the gift of prophecy and prophesied over me one day saying that I was going to be a 'cherry picker' of women, that because of my testimony, God was going to use me to pick many women for the Kingdom. I thought to myself, women do not even like me, how are they going to receive from me? But this was God's prophecy, not mine. Then, *City Church* came to the Women's house as well and one of the pastors prophesied over my life, as well as Toney, saying we were going to get married, that we were going to have six-figure jobs, that our credit was going to be restored, and that we were going to buy homes, and have a large ministry helping people that had gone to prison, the homeless, prostitutes, those with addictions, including sexual addictions, and many more issues.

I was laughing to myself because I had filed bankruptcy twice, I was unemployed, and only had a car that I did not even own. How was any of this going to come to pass with how my life looked in the natural? I let it go and just continued with the protocol of the Women's house. I did my daily prayer and meditation in the morning, and went to Bible studies and the Church. I poured myself even more into helping the women so I reached out to *Christ's Church* and a woman named Dani, who was my next angel. She helped me put on a baby shower for the homeless women, the women in the house, and the women at *Christ the King*. Women from so many churches came and brought gifts for all of these homeless women and those struggling in our house. We also helped with the women living in the local hotels.

Even though I was serving and helping others as a Christian woman, I still felt like I had this huge X on my body, like I still did not "fit" with other Christian women. The closest I ever felt to other Christian women was when I moved into the Women's house because we had all come out of many of the same circumstances. I did not understand the concept that each and every one of us needs Jesus the same, no matter where we come from or what we experience in our individual lives. But here I am with this beautiful angel, Dani, and I do not feel like I belong anywhere near her. She is a middle class woman, a mother of four, her husband is a policeman, and they go to a very upstanding church in upper middle class Federal Way. There was no place there for a woman like me. I wanted to be; I desperately desired to be; because they had so much good training, counseling, and all kinds of things that I really needed. I just did not think I would ever fit at this church.

The Women's house was good but there was always a lot of drama, backbiting, gossip, and people getting loaded or fornicating, whatever they weren't supposed to be doing. The women started to not like me anymore and brought it up to Pastor Bob that they did not want me there anymore. I had given an entire year to serving in this house and sold everything I owned to move in there. They came up with an entire "list" as to why they no longer wanted me living there. Well, Pastor Bob honored their wishes and told me I had to move out, stating they were closing the house, but that I needed to move out first. I was devastated! I felt rejected and I was confused because I was the only one in the house that was clean and sober. My pride and ego were destroyed. I still to this day have no idea why all of that happened, but I have completely forgiven them all. God has a plan even when we do not. I had to come full circle once again and look in the mirror myself. I was still living in sin; I could not blame anyone but myself. I did learn that in order to deal with sin, you have to stop, repent, and walk in the light and then teach those God puts in your path to do the same. This is with HIS Spirit and HIS Word.

"Therefore go and make disciples of all nations, baptizing them in the name of the Father and of the Son and of the Holy Spirit" Matthew 28:19, NLT.

We all sin even as saints, but there is a difference between making mistakes and living in habitual sin. I could not keep sinning and expect not to suffer the consequences of that sin. I eventually begged my daughter to let me move in with her and she said no. I couldn't even store a few boxes at her house because her place was too small. So, I could not count on any of my family members to help me. I was receiving unemployment and I still had my Toyota, so worst case scenario, I would have to sleep in my car. The Good News is that God led me to a wonderful woman named Mary. Mary lived by Toney's house and she had rooms for rent. I rented a room from her and lived with her for about a year and a quarter. Mary was a Christian, at least she stated she was, but I cannot judge another man's walk. It was pretty expensive to live there, but I could not complain as I had a roof over my head and it was a clean environment. I became very close to her family, probably as close as anyone could get in this life. I really took to her sons and loved them dearly. Toney and I became closer and we had aspirations to get married, but I knew he needed to "bake" in his program and I did not want to mess anything up for him.

I just threw myself back into serving God in any way I could, and somehow, He got my old job back for me. I began working back at the law firm and the six-figure income that was prophesied over me became a reality. I was ecstatic! Most of it was from bonuses, but it did not matter because I was never going to miss the bonus. This was now possibly going to help me to buy a new house. I was around forty-six or forty-seven at this time, and I went to *Bible Fellowship* church for a little while and started working in Des Moines. I did that for a few months and began freaking out again with anxiety, so they let me work from home. I was now building my credit and working with a mortgage lender to see about getting a home loan and I met my friend Cari. I loved Cari so much, she helped me walk through all of my fears and anxieties. The thought of buying a home was a very claustrophobic feeling for me because you cannot just simply get up and walk away, and it is a heavy responsibility.

I began to pray heavily and God helped me to get approved for my home. All of a sudden, the spirit of anxiety hit me like a ton of bricks! If I could have taken medication at that time, I absolutely would have but I chose to just work through it on my own and later with God's Word. God helped me buy a cute little condominium that was about $100,000.00 and I thought it would be great because it would be paid off by the time I was sixty. I figured me and Toney would get married and we would live in this home together for the rest of my life because I did not have any other family and my kids wanted nothing to do with me, so it would be perfect for me and Toney. Well, three days before closing, the owners pull out of the deal for some unknown reason. I was devastated once again, and the spirit of fear and anxiety came over me in full force. What was I going to do? Where was I going to go? Well, the mortgage company raised my approval amount to around $250-275,000.00 and I found this cute little rambler near Federal Way and Des Moines that was close to everything I needed and was near the water, which is something I always wanted to live near.

So, we closed on the house and the spirit of fear came over me again. I was deathly afraid to live in the house by myself, so I asked my son to move in with me. Fear of not being able to pay for it haunted me and doubts sprung up in my life as it had so many times before. I eventually got over the fear and began going to *Christ's Church*, which was up on the hill where Dani was and she invited me to sit with her and her family every Sunday. Their family was so sweet and kind to me. The pastor, Pastor Jeff, was a phenomenal preacher much more elevated than where I came from, whereas Pastor Sims served a "steak dinner" sermon, Pastor Jeff served Lobster with steak on the side and dessert! I began to learn the absolute truth and eternal security of Jesus Christ in my life. People were so nice to me but again, I did not feel like I belonged there. I felt like I was the girl with all the problems and mind you, nobody is saying any of this to me; this is just how *Susan* always felt about Susan. Selfish, self-centered, call it what you want, but I was still very broken.

The house leader from *Bible Fellowship* had gotten treatment and became sober, so I let her move in with me. She was going to come and help me while I worked and I was terrified to be alone, so it seemed like a win-win situation. Unfortunately, a month into moving in with me, she started to do drugs again. I had this man come by the house one day and ask me what I was going to do with all this room. I told him that I was going to use it to serve God, and that is exactly what I did. I allowed people to come and cut my grass that no one else would even think about bringing near their home. We began to have Bible studies, support groups, and outside church under the patio. This house was going to be a House for the Lord. I love serving in my home, but my anxiety would not let me go out and about too far. One day, I left and had a tremendous panic attack and I did not go back out for a long time. I did not go to doctors, so I did not realize that a lot of the anxiety was caused by menopause. I finally know this twelve years later.

I continued to go to church and received the refreshing of the Lord in my life. I figured this would be the next season where God would elevate the ministry within me to build houses for women and to serve in this capacity even greater. Toney was asking me every day to marry him, as we had been together at this point about four to five years. He was still in the Men's house and going to church, ministering and going out into the streets, and sharing the Gospel. Toney is now an evangelist pastor. He did not come to church that way, but God made him an evangelist pastor. God prophesied to Toney that he was going to make "camps of men" that were going to go out into the streets and share the Gospel. I will share more about this in detail with you in later chapters.

Life is still a daily fight for me; I still seem to have this dark cloud hovering over my head. I could not figure out where it continued to come from, what was causing this to linger in my life? Mind you, I was a Baptist, Calvinist, and once Catholic believer. I was not Pentecostal. I had gone to several Pentecostal churches and have some beliefs of Pentecostalism, but I am not what you would call a "Pentecostal". Meaning, I did not understand the gifts and the churches I went to didn't even believe in the gifts anymore. Eventually, I started to hang around people that did know about the gifts and who operated in them. I began to talk more about the Holy Spirit and what He meant in my life, and the Baptism of the Holy Spirit. I do believe that the moment I accepted Jesus Christ into my life, the Holy Spirit came to dwell within me. The Bible clearly shows us what takes place upon salvation and the corresponding sending of discipleship.

"For in one Spirit we were all baptized into one body—Jews or Greeks, slaves or free—and all were made to drink of one Spirit" 1 Corinthians 12:13, NKJV.

Jesus Christ is BIG! I believe that some religions, and even many theologies, tend to limit what God can do in our lives. What we need to understand is that the New Testament of the Bible is called the Dispensation of Grace, meaning we do not have to lose our lives to accept Jesus Christ. Anything after the Book of Acts is speaking of salvation because Jesus had died, risen, and fulfilled the prophecy of Isaiah and our forefathers who prophesied that Jesus would be our Messiah, our salvation. Before the ascension of Jesus Christ, He told His disciples to wait for the promise of the Holy Spirit. He told them that He must leave, in order for the Spirit of God to come and that He would be their witness to spread the Gospel to the ends of the Earth. I am not a theologian, but I clearly read in those scriptures that the Holy Spirit is, indeed, a huge part of the endtime church's assignment to spread the Gospel. The death, burial, and resurrection of Jesus Christ is the main reason to share His truth.

"No one has ever seen God, but the one and only Son, who is himself God and is in closest relationship with the Father, has made him known" John 1:18, NKJV.

I was so grateful when I came to *Christ's Church* because they had discipleship, biblical counseling, and spiritual guidance that was in line with Scripture. I had a worldly therapist and I had a biblical counselor, Dani was that biblical counselor for me. The first time she came over, I was struggling heavily with anxiety and could barely hold my Starbucks tea because I was shaking so badly. I now know there was a negative spirit that was following me in my life. I did not have the Word of God deeply implanted within me then that I needed to be able to walk through these situations to be fully delivered. This is where Dani really came in to help me. We began a study of "Trusting God[2]" by Jerry Bridges. He has passed away now, but he wrote this book in very "old English" and I can tell you that this was the best Bible study, short of the Bible, I have ever read. He explains the character of God the Father, God the Son, and God the Holy Spirit in a way you will never forget. It gave me so much peace and hope for my future that it completely changed my life. I began to learn about the things that caused me fear, and why I did not have to fear any longer. As I stated earlier, I believe fear was a generational curse that was passed down into my life through my own mother. I also learned that fear, anxiety, and panic were not of God. That I needed to learn to renew my mind with the Word of God to heal from these lies of the devil and of my horrific past.

"And so, dear brothers and sisters, I plead with you to give your bodies to God because of all he has done for you. Let them be a living and holy sacrifice—the kind he will find acceptable. This is truly the way to worship him. Don't copy the behavior and customs of this world, but let God transform you into a new person by changing the way you think. Then you will learn to know God's will for you, which is good and pleasing and perfect" Romans 12:1-2, NKJV.

Dani helped me not only through these two hour a day weekly studies, but she expressed the love of God like no one I had ever met. She was so kind, compassionate, and non-judgmental toward me. Her love for God and for me opened up my heart to be able to receive His

---

[2] Bridges, Jerry. "Trusting God". Carol Stream, IL. NavPress. 2008.

Word into my life and into my situations. I was beginning to finally heal from my past. Dani taught me to journal my feelings daily and then put off the old lying emotions and put on the truth of God's Word. All the therapy I had ever had in my life never healed those deep seated trauma's the way God could.

"Jesus said to him, "I am the way, the truth, and the life. No one comes to the Father except through Me" John 14:66, NLT.

Chapter 12

The Beginning of Ministry

"But you should keep a clear mind in every situation. Don't be afraid of suffering for the Lord. Work at telling others the Good News, and fully carry out the ministry God has given you."
2 Timothy 4:5, NLT

Me and the woman that was leading with me in the Women's house are now living in this house that God had blessed me with, and I was still struggling with horrendous anxiety and fear. I rarely left my home and when I did, I was overwhelmed the entire time. I felt like I was literally going to die in this state of mind. I was not a housewife, a cook, or a gardener. I was not domesticated at all. How was I going to take care of this home and all that came with it? I began to panic, so I put the house up for rent on Craig's List. I was going to rent it out and go back to Mary's house where I felt safe. I was willing to go backwards because I was so deathly afraid to go forward. The spirit of fear had so entrapped me because it did not want me to move forward in my life. This woman was nice enough to move in with me and she helped me to cook and clean, and helped to take care of me due to my obesity. The psychiatrist would called it PTSD (Post Traumatic Stress Disorder) to make me feel better when in reality, the devil had me bound and stuck in my home, not able to function like I would have wanted to function. I was also in a great state of depression.

I was forty-eight years old at this time and had no clue what menopause was like, but I was obviously in the beginning stages of it. My periods began to get erratic with some months of heavy flowing and others where it was literally nothing for several months. I was deathly afraid of cancer and the possibility of a hysterectomy, along with the anxiety and fear. My entire emotional and mental state was out of control at this point. I would pray daily that He would get me through all of these things happening simultaneously in my life. I truly felt like the woman with the issue of blood, if I could just touch the hem of His garment, I would be made whole.

"And suddenly, a woman who had a flow of blood for twelve years came from behind and touched the hem of His garment. For she said to herself, "If only I may touch His garment, I shall be made well." But Jesus turned around, and when He saw her He said, "Be of good cheer, daughter; your faith has made you well." And the woman was made well from that hour" Matthew 9:20-22, NKJV.

I just knew that God was going to give me what I needed. We must understand that sometimes, God is not going to heal us on this side of Heaven, whether that is physically, emotionally, mentally, or otherwise. This is a very tough reality for some Christian believers. Even though I couldn't leave like I wanted to, and I was struggling immensely with fear and anxiety, I still believed God. I didn't want to end up like Peter denying Christ, and though Paul was one of the most faith-filled apostles, he still had a "thorn" in his flesh.

2 Corinthians 12:7-10 (NLT) says, *"... even though I have received such wonderful revelations from God. So to keep me from becoming proud, I was given a thorn in my flesh, a messenger from Satan to torment me and keep me from becoming proud. Three different times I begged the Lord to take it away. Each time he said, "My grace is all you need. My power works best in weakness." So now I am glad to boast about my weaknesses, so that the power of Christ can work through me. That's why I take pleasure in my weaknesses, and in the insults, hardships, persecutions, and troubles that I suffer for Christ. For when I am weak, then I am strong."*

God's grace was sufficient for me, and I had to get to some kind of place of grasping and understanding this most crucial truth in my life. My husband and I have this joke that we say about the Dispensation of Grace. There will be a time on the Earth after this dispensation ends where those that want to accept Jesus Christ as their Lord and Savior will be martyred, they will literally have their heads cut off at their necks. It is not going to be a fun, easy way to accept the Lord. Our joke is that if we would be living in that dispensation, my husband's neck would be on the block so fast that it would make your head spin. He would not care if they took his head. Me, I would be on my scooter racing down the street. This is the spirit of fear in operation.

"For God has not given us a spirit of fear, but of power and of love and of a sound mind" 2 Timothy 1:7, NKJV.

This is why we know the spirit of fear is not real, that it is not of God. We have the power through Christ to cast out any demon, whether it is fear, anxiety, depression, or anything that is contrary to God's thoughts about you. He not only provides us with power, love, and a sound mind, but He also offers us His peace to overcome any and all attacks from Satan.

"And the God of peace will crush Satan under your feet shortly. The grace of our Lord Jesus Christ be with you. Amen" Romans 16:20, NKJV.

I had begun to use the Word of God daily to combat my feelings. Pastor Sims used to teach us, "Don't let your feelings get higher than your faith." I used to wonder what this meant. At that time, my faith was not that great and I had more feelings than an Amtrak train. I was always emotional for some reason, traumatized, and heartbroken at every crossroad, mostly concerning my kids and my past life. The devil was continuing to dig and dig into my emotions. He is truly the accuser of the brethren. He accuses us before the throne of God day and night.

"Then I heard a loud voice shouting across the heavens, "It has come at last—salvation and power and the Kingdom of our God, and the authority of his Christ. For the accuser of our brothers and sisters has been thrown down to earth—the one who accuses them before our God day and night" Revelation 12:10, NLT.

We have to understand that our fight is not against flesh and blood, and not even against our mind, will, and emotions, and the harsh circumstances we are faced with in our lives. It is against things and entities not of this world. I was constantly in a battle with something all throughout my entire life. At every turn, I would be in the fight for my life; at times, literally. We have a real enemy and it is not other people and certainly not even ourselves, it is our true enemy, the evil one, the devil... Satan himself!

"For we do not wrestle against flesh and blood, but against principalities, against powers, against the rulers of the darkness of this age, against spiritual hosts of wickedness in the heavenly places" Ephesians 6:12, NKJV.

Crazy enough, though I always seemed to be in some sort of battle, I always felt the Light of God. From a biblical standpoint and even in regard to my feelings and emotions, I could always feel God with me. I know the Holy Spirit lives within me because there is a peace that continually follows me, it remains with me, no matter what I am facing. I know that is where the truth is held within me, in my soul. Sometimes, that peace may seem very quiet and not so evident, because my flesh is screaming louder, not trusting what I know the Word says concerning me. The battle is truly in our minds, as Elyse Fitzpatrick and other biblical counselors say in their books. Ephesians 4:22-24 below states to throw off your old sinful nature and your former way of life, and the only way to achieve this is by the Grace and Power of our Lord and Savior Jesus Christ (Holy Spirit), especially in the statement, "What would Jesus do?" I began journaling to help cope with my anxiety and to change my mind to the Word of God.

"... throw off your old sinful nature and your former way of life, which is corrupted by lust and deception. Instead, let the Spirit renew your thoughts and attitudes. Put on your new nature, created to be like God—truly righteous and holy," NKJV.

At this point in my life, I was really searching how I could get myself out of my house. I literally wanted to run from that house because in my mind, to own a home meant that there was only one thing left to do, and that was to die. Of course, we all are going to physically die someday no matter if we are living in a home, on the streets, or in a motel somewhere, but my thoughts and the mental state I was in caused me to believe I was living in a prison in this home. I know that I am never going to die, spiritually, that I have an eternal home in Heaven with God.

"Yes, we are fully confident, and we would rather be away from these earthly bodies, for then we will be at home with the Lord" 2 Corinthians 5:8, NLT.

I simply believe the Word of God. Everything that I have gone through, am going through, or will ever go through in my life, there is Scripture that is my remedy. I did not know this in the beginning; I did not have this knowledge until much later on in my life. You must get into the Word of God and get these truths embedded within your spirit, so you can lean on them when the hard times come, and they most certainly will come. I make this joke about myself, calling myself a "Bap-Costal". I am a Baptist and a Pentecostal. What I mean by this is that I allow the Holy Spirit to show me His Word and I interpret it through concordances, online resources, and through people God has placed within my life who are learned in biblical studies and theology who have been studying the Bible their entire lives. The Bible says we must study to show ourselves approved by God. We must desire to know His Word at all costs. I also deeply believe in the Gifts of the Spirit and those God has entrusted to carry His anointing in those areas. These are other ways He can use to speak to us and through us if they remain pure.

I do know that there are some that use these gifts, specifically prophecy, for manipulation and surely, God is not pleased. I do not believe in making a mockery of God. We need to be very careful and be sure that those operating in these gifts have a firm foundation of the Word of God implanted in their hearts.

"Do not be deceived, God is not mocked; for whatever a man sows, that he will also reap" Galatians 6:7, NKJV.

I never want to be in a position of mocking God. The greatest gift God ever gave me, and it was again administered through Pastor Andre Sims, was when he came into a conference one day on a Saturday. I was so excited like I was in a concert I have never seen before, because I was like a sponge when it came to the Word of God. I would just sit there and soak it all in. I was desperately seeking hope and relief, and I wanted a better life for myself. I wanted to be able to teach my kids about God. I wanted God with all my heart, soul, mind, and strength, and I wanted to love my neighbor as myself. He came out and pointed to us saying, "You better quit worrying about what that joker thinks about you, and start worrying about what God thinks about you." That was the exact moment where God changed my entire life, my thoughts, my feelings, my emotions, and my perspective concerning not only God, but also me. All of a sudden, I began to truly care only about what He thought of me and not being a people pleaser of men, which I had been my entire life because of the spirit of fear. This caused me to make horrible decisions based upon what other people thought of me, or wanted from me.

I decided to start a Bible Study. I said well, if I was going to be in the house, I was not going to let the devil keep me all the way down. I was going to get the support I needed, and I was going to give others what

God had given to me. So, we started Bible studies and a lady in the neighborhood named Mary would help me get there. She was a mature woman of God. I was going to *Christ's Church* now, and it was a struggle but I made it happen. The Word of God here was just as good as *Christ the King*, if not better. Pastor Jeff Moorehead is one of the most amazing pastors I have ever met. He is honest and humble, and he doesn't even want you to call him "pastor". He is a teacher and a lover of the Word of God. He really cares about what God's Word says, and he really wants people to hear the truth. But most importantly, he knows GOD is GOD and he points you to God, not to him. I will be eternally grateful for *Christ the King Bible Fellowship* and *Christ's Church*, and the Pastors who minister to my life.

I continued going to *Christ's Church* and sitting with my friend Dani who I met when I was attending *Christ the King Church*. She befriended me and continued counseling me. They had a wonderful biblical counseling program and it was free. This was a win-win situation because money was an issue for me at this time. God was blessing me and I was able to work from home, and I was making a decent enough salary to pay my mortgage and have a little left over to do what I needed to do, just not enough to run an entire ministry. The other woman was still living with me at this time, but I began to get an inclination that she may very well have been using drugs again. I would bring it up to her, but she would somehow convince me that she wasn't using it anymore. My gut told me otherwise, but I was terrified to be alone. I just simply could not do some things on my own.

At this point, I still was waiting on God to decide if I wanted to marry Toney. He would ask me every single day of my life for six years if I would marry him. Toney had wanted to be a pastor so bad, even as far back as six years old. This is a sweet little story I will tell about my husband. He was raised in the projects of Florida in a very poor environment. I will let him reveal further what happened to him in his childhood, but many horrific things happened to him as a child. There is not one baby picture to be found of my husband. I have only one picture of him at the age of eighteen and he is with his friend, Jeff Blackshear, a former NFL football player. Jeff is with Jesus now. Toney had one outfit that he had at six years old that he used to wear to go to church, and his little church shoes. He would wear his little church suit every day walking around the projects and the apartment complex he lived in, and talk about Jesus.

Toney would come and visit me after leaving the women's house, and we were both dealing with so many things in our individual lives. He was still living in the men's house and I truly believed that is exactly where he needed to be to get his life together. I did not want to pull him out of a program that was truly helping his soul. Toney had gotten heavily involved in evangelism. He was feeding the homeless and taking care of people on the streets. Sharing the Gospel had become very prevalent in his life, as this is what God had called him to do. He would read the Word of God upwards of twelve to thirteen hours a day. The house that he lived at had a big twelve foot cross outside in the grass by a creek. It was so beautiful. We would sit down at that creek and just pray together. He would lay on the ground in the grass in front of that cross and ask God for His will to be done in his life. Toney is one of the most humble men of God I have ever met in my entire life.

We were having Bible Study at my home for women, at this time. I was still trying to acclimate myself to the church culture, as I still, deep down inside, felt like a prostitute. I still felt like a big, fat loser who did not parent my children right and gave one away for adoption. I still felt like the thrown away black sheep of my family because they didn't want to have anything to do with me. I still felt pretty tainted at this point. I really didn't have much treatment from the horrific things I had experienced from my late teens well into my thirties. From all of the abuse and the trauma, I was carrying a lot. I was truly searching out for help. One that I wasn't doing, and I will never do, was taking any antidepressants. I had many doctors to prescribe them and to tell me that it would help my condition, but it was just not for me. I did not have a chemical imbalance, I was suffering with a spiritual disparity. I don't have anything against people taking what they need to consume for their personal medical needs; I am just saying that I knew wholeheartedly that my issue was spiritual. It was 100% a sin issue. I had a heart full of sin. I had a bitter heart, a broken heart. The Bible says that God is close to the brokenhearted.

"The Lord is close to the brokenhearted; he rescues those whose spirits are crushed" Psalm 34:18, NLT.

God was always close to me. I knew He was with me, but I still woke up many days full of frustration. I was unhappy because I could not leave my home and my life was not what I wanted it to be. I could not sleep and was full of anxiety, and probably needed medication, but I would use chamomile tea and my friend was with me to help me. I was scared about the future, and terrified about figuring out how to take care of this home I had purchased. My faith was still very small and my trust in God was not where it should be at this point in my life. This was surely not God's fault, but my lack of faith in Him. So, I took Dani up on her offer for biblical counseling and she told me to go to the church office and fill out the paperwork and someone would be in touch with me.

One night, me and my friend were sitting in the house and this wonderful couple from *Christ's Church* showed up to meet with me. I was feeling a little bit better that I was going to receive help, I had more hope at this point. Unfortunately, I sat for an hour dumping my entire life story on these people believing they were my counselors, but they were part of the family care ministry just coming to check up on me. Boy, did I feel awkward but these precious people were so kind and did not judge me one bit. I, on the other hand, had judged them based upon my own insecurities and past experiences with people that just threw me away. It was a natural instinct for me to put up walls and to block people from getting too close to me, because I had this long standing idea that everyone would leave me. I judged them based upon their ethnicity and lifestyles, as many of them lived in a very good part of the city, Marine Hills, or in other wealthy parts of Federal Way. They had homes their entire lives with beautiful gardens, they knew how to cook, and had beautiful life groups. Their lives were beautiful to me and I simply did not know how to fit in with these people. I did not grow up like them, and I certainly was not going to learn how to live or act like them overnight. So, how was I going to fit in?

The counseling sessions were great and I began to learn so much from Dani. I learned about the character and attributes of God and how He is truly the BOSS! I was beginning to experience the peeling away of layers and layers of unhealthy and toxic thinking that had consumed my life. I learned that God is Omnipotent, Omnipresent, and Omniscient, He was all-sustaining. He was here before anything and anyone; He did not need us, He chose us. This concept alone changed my entire perspective on life. I cannot fully explain how much peace and love I gained from this truth being revealed to me.

Another breathtaking revelation I received was that God is always on the throne. He never changes; He is the same yesterday, today, and forevermore. This is a truth that is able to ground us and settle us in our thinking and in our faith in Him. This scripture alone will bring us the absolute peace we need to navigate through this ever changing world.

"Jesus Christ is the same yesterday, today, and forever" Hebrews 13:8, NKJV.

I learned that He does not sleep nor slumber, so all those nights that I was up and could not sleep, He was still right there with me. Even to this day, I have times like this where the spirit of fear wants to creep in to destroy my life, but God is right there, waiting for me to call upon His name and to receive His peace, comfort, and strength. He wants us to come to Him in those times of great need, distress, and uncertainty, so we are able to shift our thoughts from negative thinking and on to His Word and His truth.

"Finally, brethren, whatever things are true, whatever things are noble, whatever things are just, whatever things are pure, whatever things are lovely, whatever things are of good report, if there is any virtue and if there is anything praiseworthy—meditate on these things" Philippians 4:8, NKJV.

I had never heard of this scripture before Dani gave it to me. I had heard of the scripture two verses prior to "be anxious for nothing..." (Philippians 4:6) and I have to be honest, it made me very mad because I did not want to be anxious. I had no idea what was causing it and I simply wanted God to take it away! I didn't understand that above and beyond the chemical imbalances going on in my brain, along with the hormonal imbalances and menopausal symptoms, I had a spirit of fear following me that did not belong to God that was wreaking havoc in my life. I had to learn how to pray with supplication. I did not know what supplication meant, so as I began to research; I found that it means the action of asking or begging for something earnestly or humbly. Now, this is the natural meaning, but it shines some light on the manner in which we are to continue petitioning, or appealing, to God for the things that we are seeking. We don't have to necessarily beg God to heal us, or for the things we need in our lives, but He does desire for us to come to Him in every situation that we are in need and to come as often as we need to do so. God may not heal our bodies or heal us from anxiety or fear on this side of Heaven, but we are to continuously, while we are still on this Earth, seek Him for it. This is faith!

"Now faith is the substance of things hoped for, the evidence of things not seen" Hebrews 11:1, NKJV.

Hope is truly the key to holding on to the promises of God. If you have hope, you can wait for forty years for something you have asked Him for because you understand that everything is in His timing and that He works all things together for the good of those that love Him and for those who are called according to His purpose. The Bible says we can have faith the size of a mustard seed, which is one of the smallest seeds on the Earth, and subsequently move mountains and that nothing will be impossible for us. He simply desires for us to seek Him with all of our hearts. He wants us to come to Him and fellowship with Him in intimacy. God desires to provide a future for us with hope (Jeremiah 29:11).

I am always seeking God in some way. I may not always be walking as I am supposed to be, but one thing I love about Him is that He does not require us to work for His love. But we must also understand that we are not to take His grace for granted. Our hope lies within Christ and the only way for us to experience the abundant life in Him, we must be born again. Not one of us is born automatically into the Kingdom of God, even if we are born into a Christian family. Each one of us has to believe in our hearts that God raised Jesus from the dead and confess that He is Lord. Each one of us must repent before Him and seek the Kingdom of God. Our faith must be in Him and Him alone. We can have faith for certain things in our lives and in this world, but only faith in Him is able to save our souls for eternity. I don't care what religion you are currently apart of, if they tell you there is another way to enter Heaven, the Kingdom, or Paradise, they are lying to you. Jesus is the Only Way and He is the Only One that is able to reconcile us back to the Father.

"For God in all his fullness was pleased to live in Christ, and through him God reconciled everything to himself. He made peace with everything in heaven and on earth by means of Christ's blood on the cross" Colossians 1:19-20, NLT.

We have to be reconciled back to Him due to our sinful nature. He gives us free will; He is not going to force Himself upon us. Somewhere in your life, you are going to hear the Truth of God's Word at least once, if not many times. He chose you; you did not choose Him. Someone is going to share the Gospel with you in your lifetime. I want to end this chapter by sharing the glorious Gospel of our Lord Jesus Christ with you. Many people will say, "I can't help it; I am this way, I was born that way." Well, that is true, we were all born of sin but the goal of reconciliation is to become like Christ. The Book of Ephesians chapter 1 will tell you who you are in Christ, don't allow the world to define who you are. In the 70's, there were a ton of self-help books on "finding out who you are". These are wasted reads, when God wrote who you are many, many years ago in HIS Word.

In Romans 3:21-26 (NKJV), it says:

*"But now the righteousness of God apart from the law is revealed, being witnessed by the Law and the Prophets, even the righteousness of God, **through faith in Jesus Christ, to all and on all who believe**. For there is no difference; **for all have sinned and fall short of the glory of God**, being justified freely by His grace through the redemption that is in Christ Jesus, whom God set forth as a propitiation by His blood, through faith, to demonstrate His righteousness, because in His forbearance God had passed over the sins that were previously committed, to demonstrate at the present time His righteousness, **that He might be just and the justifier of the one who has faith in Jesus"***
(emphasis).

God loves us so very much and He desires for us to choose Him, to choose His Son Jesus whom He sent to die on the Cross for the redemption of our sins. He died a gruesome death with His flesh stripped from His body, so you and I could live forever in eternity with Him. He presented His Blood before the throne of God, so we could be received as pure and holy by the Father. Not one of us is good enough to make it to Heaven on our own. God is holy. God is pure. Sin cannot dwell in His Presence; therefore, Jesus had to become the Atonement for our sin, so we could be reconciled back to the Father. Jesus is God who came in the flesh, and now sits at the right hand of the Father in Spirit interceding for us. He is all good. He is all love. He is all light. He is all truth. We must receive Him to be holy, as He is holy.

No matter who you are, or what you have gone through in your life, Jesus loves you! Your sin, no matter how evil or wicked, can be washed and cleansed by the Lord. There is not one person on the face of the Earth that is born "good". The Bible says we are all wicked and our hearts deceitful. I don't care how good someone thinks they are; apart from God, we are sinful, deceitful, and wicked. Outside of Christ, I am a wretched woman.

"The heart is deceitful above all things, And desperately wicked; Who can know it?" Jeremiah 17:9, NKJV.

No one can love you like God, not your husband, your wife, your boyfriend, your girlfriend, your pimp, your drug supplier, your bookie, or anyone that is mere flesh! I truly thought my pimps loved me, but they did not die on the Cross for me! Anyone can let us down in this world, but God will never let us down. He will never leave us or forsake us. His love is settled in Heaven, it is His Word... Jesus Christ, the Son of the Living God! He is love personified! May we continue to develop a healthy fear, reverence, honor, and awe for Him in our lives. Not a fear of being scared of Him, because as He said, He has not given us a spirit of fear, but of absolute power, love, and a sound mind. But an advantageous, reverential fear is what leads us to wisdom in all things. His wisdom, not our own.

"The fear of the Lord is the beginning of wisdom; A good understanding have all those who do His commandments. His praise endures forever" Psalm 111:10, NKJV.

On the Fourth of July when we sit to see the fireworks, we will hear the "ooooo's and ahhhh's" of the crowd as they look up and see the magnificent display of lights in the night sky. This is the awe that we should constantly seek to have of our Father in Heaven. Not a day should go by that we don't recognize His glory in our lives and in the Earth. As we fear His Sovereignty, reverence His Holiness, honor His Word, and keep His commandments, we can stand boldly in awe of His magnificent glory and praise His Name, for He is Worthy to be Praised!!!

God's grace and mercy is readily available to each and every one of us that will call upon His name. Grace is getting something you don't deserve and mercy is not getting what you do deserve. I can tell you that I deserve death for all of the things I have done in my life. There are so many things that I have thought and said and felt that I did not deserve the grace, or the mercy, God provided for me. But He gave it anyway. This is how much He loves us! He loved us while we were yet sinners!

"But God demonstrates His own love toward us, in that while we were still sinners, Christ died for us" Romans 5:8, NKJV.

Receive Him into your life today!

Chapter 13

The Truth that Heals

"And you shall know the truth, and the truth shall make you free."
John 8:32, NKJV

Addictions are not a simple thing to break in people's lives. It is easy to think, or say, that all someone has to do is put down the bottle, turn off the computer, stay away from the streets, close the refrigerator, or put down the pipe. Addiction is not a surface-level issue, it stems from very deeply rooted strongholds, traumas, and abuses in people's childhoods and even into adulthood. I was an alcoholic, a drug addict, a prostitute, a gambler, a cigarette smoker, and I still struggle with gluttony and compulsive overeating, which I am working on till this day with a doctor as it has become so severe. Sin will kill you, but we need to learn how to come out of the darkness and into His marvelous light. We cannot continue to make excuses for our addictions, our sin, or we will remain in them and ultimately, die in them.

We cannot place the blame on something, or someone, that happened years ago and this is the reason we are still battling with addiction.

Someone hurt you, so to get rid of the pain, you go and get loaded. I can remember one time vividly when I drank and did drugs; I was sitting in a park after I had gone through with an abortion. I was utterly devastated because, as a Catholic, I had committed the mortal sin of killing a baby, in my mind. I had taken down about six cans of beer, but it was no longer covering the pain, the guilt, and the shame, and let me just be honest, it really never did. It was just the lie I believed from the devil. These were spirits, demons, that I had allowed to consume my life just so I could ease the pain, but in essence, I was causing greater damage and destruction that would steal years from my life.

I want to dampen the lies that alcoholics tell themselves, believing that they will never be able to climb out of that pit of alcoholism. You can do anything you want, one day at a time. Anything that you need to do to take care of yourself, you can do so with the power of God in your life. Every twenty-four hour day of your life, for the rest of your life, you can do great things and take great strides if you surrender yourself to Him and cry out to the Lord for help.

"The temptations in your life are no different from what others experience. And God is faithful. He will not allow the temptation to be more than you can stand. When you are tempted, he will show you a way out so that you can endure" 1 Corinthians 10:13, NLT.

God's desire is to deliver you, just as He delivered me and many others from the destruction of alcohol and other devastating addictions. We all have sinned; not one of us is without it, or exempt from it. But just as the above scripture states, *"God is faithful,* who will not allow you to be tempted beyond what you are able;" there is a remedy to your recovery, an answer for your addiction, and help for your healing, just as it was for me. His name… Jesus! He is Jehovah Rapha, the Lord your Healer! He is Jehovah Mekkodishkim, the Lord who sanctifies you! He is truly our Great Physician! It goes on further to say that *He will also make the way of escape for us, that we may be able to bear it.* Oh, what love!!! There is absolutely nothing we cannot overcome with the Lord on our side.

"Yet in all these things we are more than conquerors through Him who loved us" Romans 8:37, NKJV.

Yes, we are now a new creation in Christ, but this is not going to happen overnight for most people. Sanctification is a process from the day you accept Jesus, until the Day He returns to get you to make you eternally perfect! We are, indeed, going to be perfect one day, because He is going to wipe away all of the sin, all of the tears, all of the hurt, all of the pain, all of the betrayal, all of the abuse, all of the trauma, and yes, all of the sickness, disease, and addictions in our lives. We are going to walk in absolute freedom in our eternal home with our Lord. I would love to be able to experience that freedom on this Earth at some point. A lot of people do not believe this is possible, but His Word says otherwise.

"Now to Him who is able to do exceedingly abundantly above all that we ask or think, according to the power that works in us, to Him be glory in the church by Christ Jesus to all generations, forever and ever. Amen" Ephesians 3:20-21, NKJV.

It is truly His power working within us that allows us to break free from the addictions we suffer within this life, but we just have to believe. But there is also something we have to do for ourselves in the area of deliverance from these addictions, and that is to receive accountability. You must seek out and surround yourself with mature believers that can not only share with you the Word of God for your situation, but also hold you accountable to the Word and walk with you through to the other side.

"Brethren, if a man is overtaken in any trespass, you who are spiritual restore such a one in a spirit of gentleness, considering yourself lest you also be tempted" Galatians 6:1, NKJV.

Please, do not get offended at the word "sin;" we all have things we are struggling with, simply let God heal you. Sin is designed to destroy us, and many times in our addictions, we are so numb from our pain that we do not realize that we have an enemy that wants us dead! In Alcoholics Anonymous, I learned that women are considered last stage alcoholics after drinking continuously for seven years; for men, fourteen years. There were no treatment programs for a seventeen year old girl at that time in AA. They told me to go to 90 meetings in 90 days, and 120 meetings in 120 days. I was told to "change my playground!" Folks, change your playground!!! They say in Alcoholics Anonymous that the only hope for an alcoholic is prison, institutions, and death. I used to believe this, until I gave my life to Jesus. I now know that my hope is in Christ, in His willingness to draw me closer to Him. His willingness to die on a cross to save me from my sin.

Remember, we all have free will and God will not push, pry, or try to move past that free will to get us to change our lifestyle choices or the habitual patterns, cycles, or addictions we have allowed into our lives. But, when we accept Him into our lives through salvation, deliverance is absolutely available for God's children. The Bible clarifies this in

Matthew 15 revealing that deliverance is "the children's bread;" it is our birthright as children of God, in the Kingdom of God.

Speaking to the alcoholic and the addict, working the steps is very important but there is a book by Celebrate Recovery that has comparison with the steps to scriptures in the Bible. We don't want to get too far away from the truth in order to heal. The recovery rate in Celebrate Recovery is much higher than Alcoholics Anonymous. We have to recognize the truth and reality in this statement. The Word of God truly works. At my worst and most broken, I knew I needed to fear the Lord and have a foundation that I could stand upon, or I was not going to make it. The second thing that was wrong with my spirit, my soul, and my person, my greatest hindrance, was that I got offended by some of the most insignificant things anyone would say to me. If I did not like what you were saying to me, I would turn you off and not listen to you. Whether it was true or not, it did not matter because you hurt my feelings. I almost let that concept and crutch destroy my entire life.

"Whoever loves instruction loves knowledge, But he who hates correction is stupid" Proverbs 12:1, NKJV.

We have to get tough and look in the mirror and decide that we will go to any lengths to get these demons off of our backs! Whether it is alcohol, drugs, sexual addiction, gambling, smoking, food, or whatever it is you are struggling or battling with in your life. Faith without works is dead. We have to make a determined decision that we no longer desire to live these lifestyles of destruction and death, because that is exactly the path we are heading down if we do not turn around quickly. We have to seek out wise counsel. We have to allow people to correct us for us to get better. It is called being humble. It is called being submissive to the

Lord in the process to your healing and deliverance. I am forty-one years sober and I have had to submit to my own process to get to this point in my life. I had to submit to the Lord and to His Word to understand what my inheritance was in Christ, and to find my identity in Him.

When we refuse to submit and to receive, claiming that our feelings are hurt or that someone offended us, we are allowing entrance for lies and deception to enter our lives. Feelings will lie to you! I am not saying feelings aren't important or that you should neglect the feelings and emotions that you have from walking through some very traumatic experiences in your life. I am speaking of the lies that tell you that there is no hope whatsoever for you to be healed and delivered from those traumas. There is always hope in Jesus Christ.

"And I am convinced that nothing can ever separate us from God's love. Neither death nor life, neither angels nor demons, neither our fears for today nor our worries about tomorrow—not even the powers of hell can separate us from God's love" Romans 8:38, NLT.

God loves us with an undying love, but we have to accept it. We have to first receive His love, then He will provide us with the wisdom, knowledge, and understanding to heal and to get well. Then, we must do our part and seek out the avenues to stay well. We have our own part to play in our deliverance. God wants us to be well. We must stop drinking, stop popping pills, stop smoking, stop shooting heroin, stop prostituting, stop giving a pimp your money that is beating you and killing you, stop gambling, stop the secret sexual addiction, stop the compulsive overeating and gluttony, and stop participating in any sinful acts that are designed to destroy your life. God wants you healed and delivered for two reasons: one, because He loves you with an everlasting love, and because He desires to reconcile you to Himself. He is not an evil or wicked God. He is a good Father! The second reason is that He has given us gifts to build His Kingdom. Not only the Gifts of the Spirit, but also the Fruit of the Spirit.

"There are diversities of gifts, but the same Spirit. There are differences of ministries, but the same Lord. And there are diversities of activities, but it is the same God who works all in all. But the manifestation of the Spirit is given to each one for the profit of all: for to one is given the word of wisdom through the Spirit, to another the word of knowledge through the same Spirit, to another faith by the same Spirit, to another gifts of healings by the same Spirit, to another the working of miracles, to another prophecy, to another discerning of spirits, to another different kinds of tongues, to another the interpretation of tongues. But one and the same Spirit works all these things, distributing to each one individually as He wills" 1 Corinthians 12:4-11, NKJV.

"The Spirit of the Lord shall rest upon Him, The Spirit of wisdom and understanding, The Spirit of counsel and might, The Spirit of knowledge and of the fear of the Lord" Isaiah 11:2-3, NKJV.

"Having then gifts differing according to the grace that is given to us, let us use them: if prophecy, let us prophesy in proportion to our faith; or ministry, let us use it in our ministering; he who teaches, in teaching; he who exhorts, in exhortation; he who gives, with liberality; he who leads, with diligence; he who shows mercy, with cheerfulness" Romans 12:6-8, NKJV.

"And He Himself gave some to be apostles, some prophets, some evangelists, and some pastors and teachers, for the equipping of the saints for the work of ministry, for the edifying of the body of Christ" Ephesians 4:11-12, NKJV.

"But the fruit of the Spirit is love, joy, peace, longsuffering, kindness, goodness, faithfulness, gentleness, self-control. Against such there is no law" Galatians 5:22-23, NKJV.

All of these scriptures provide us the ammunition and tools to walk through every test, every trial, and every tribulation we will ever face in this life. We can be encouraged, equipped, and empowered through the Word of God to come out of the darkness and into His marvelous light, with His Word in our mouths and our testimonies on our lips.

There are so many ways to get help these days for those with addiction. I am from the old school Alcoholics Anonymous and drug addiction programs. Number one, admit you have a problem with alcohol, drugs, or whatever your struggle may be, and that it is out of hands. At this point, you are no longer in control of what is going on in your life. It has completely taken you over, and is destroying you. Stop letting doctors convince you that you need Suboxone or Methadone to heal. God is big enough to take away your cravings and renew your life. But you have to walk in this daily and the footwork is on you. Don't pick up the first drug, drink, food, gambling habit, cigarette, sexual sin, or whatever is your issue. It is really that simple, because God is BIG enough to give you the grace to survive your cravings. It is your best friend and your hated enemy. Secondly, come to believe that a power greater than yourself can come to restore you to sanity. You have to get to a place in your life where Jesus is able to heal you, deliver you, and set you free from the trauma, torment, and torture that these addictions have unleashed upon you. You have to be willing with the faith of a mustard seed to believe God is big enough to change your sick mind. You will come to know and experience this as you read, study, and meditate upon His Word. It is like a double-edged sword; God's power is in His Word and in His Spirit. It has the capacity to cut through the hardest of places within us, like as skilled surgeon, to get to those cancerous areas to remove them from our lives.

"For the word of God is alive and powerful. It is sharper than the sharpest two-edged sword, cutting between soul and spirit, between joint and marrow. It exposes our innermost thoughts and desires" Hebrews 4:12, NLT.

You may think that no one understands what you are going through or that no one is able to help you heal because your addiction is so far gone. I am here to tell you that God is the ONLY One who can see into the depths of our soul and our spirit, and is able to pierce through those indestructible walls and barriers that the enemy has erected in our lives through past abuse, trauma, and pain. Addictions only come due to these traumas; they start out as "band-aids" to cover up gaping wounds but they will not stick, they will not stop the bleeding. You will find yourself layering those bandages with addiction upon addiction, until you find yourself so far deep in the darkest pits of hell that you cannot find your way out. But there is hope! That hope is in Jesus Christ! God brings you accountability partners that you need to glean from; be honest with yourself daily and stay busy with His purpose for you. Be content where you are, so He can take you to the next level of your life. TRUST HIM WITH ALL YOUR HEART… allow Christ to be formed within you.

"For God wanted them to know that the riches and glory of Christ are for you Gentiles, too. And this is the secret: Christ lives in you. This gives you assurance of sharing his glory" Colossians 1:27, NLT.

I was so eternally grateful that God had pulled me out of the darkest pits in my life: the fear, the anxiety, the depression, the thoughts of suicide, the guilt, the shame... I was in the prison of my soul. Unfortunately, at that time, I would continue to add layer upon layer of addiction trying to cover up each trauma I was facing. This was my only coping mechanism because I knew no other way. I never really "lived" my life during those years. I was merely existing, day by day, minute by minute, second by second. I never had vacations or traveled with family to other countries. I never really celebrated holidays or birthdays like most normal families do, I have always been in *survival mode*. God changed all of that for me and began to show me His thoughts toward me, and began to impart His perfect will into my life. I began to believe more and more of His plans to prosper me and for the hope and future He designed for my life. I knew He was with me and that He would never leave me.

"Be strong and of good courage, do not fear nor be afraid of them; for the Lord your God, He is the One who goes with you. He will not leave you nor forsake you" Deuteronomy 31:6, NKJV.

I absolutely understand that some people may need to take medication if they have chemical imbalances, or other more severe mental issues that may warrant taking pharmaceuticals. For me, I had so many issues that were compounded in my life due to my childhood trauma and fear that I wanted to get to the root of before I made the decision to take medications to numb the issues. I researched heavily on these medications to find out what they did for the symptoms, as well as the side effects that I would face taking them. There is a book called "Blame it on the Brain[3]" that speaks of bipolar disorder and schizophrenia and it explains in detail what these diagnoses are and how to combat them in your life. If you are struggling in these areas, this book will help you tremendously. I found that these two specific diagnoses are the only disorders that absolutely require medications to function normally. Now, can God heal you of these, absolutely! But there is a faithful saying, "Until He does, take your medication!" If you are hearing voices and your chemical imbalances are causing you to be up and down and all over the place, you cannot be useful to the Kingdom of God.

But even in those times, God is with you and holding your hand, healing your heart, wiping your tears, giving you hope, restoring your mind, reconciling you back to Him, and placing His gifts within you to help build His Kingdom in the Earth. You are needed! Don't ever let anyone tell you that because you struggle with any kind of addiction that God cannot use you, or that you cannot be used by Him until you are completely healed and free of those addictions. God says come to Me as you are, I love you and accept you. He did not come to condemn you, but to save you.

"For God did not send His Son into the world to condemn the world, but that the world through Him might be saved" John 3:17, NKJV.

---

[3] Welch, Edward T. "Blame it on the Brain". Phillipsburg, NJ. P & R Publishing. 1998.

Not one person on the face of this Earth has the right or authority to judge you. If He didn't, and does not, then you keep on seeking Him and putting your trust in Him and not man. He knows your most intimate thoughts and struggles and still says you are His! He sees every hurt, pain, disappointment, abuse, betrayal, and act committed against you and still says you are priceless to Him. It is in Him that we live, we move, and we have our very being. I am here as a witness, shouting from the mountaintops, that HE IS GOD… JESUS IS GOD!!! He is everything that you will ever need. This life will never be perfect, but HE is perfect; therefore, He is able to help us walk through this world in love, peace, and joy in the Holy Spirit. The Bible says we are in this world, but not of it; meaning first, when we accept Jesus Christ as our Lord and Savior, we immediately enter the Kingdom of Heaven. The Bible says we are "seated with Him in heavenly places;" we now can operate in both realms. Secondly, though we are in this evil and wicked world, we do not have to walk as the world walks in chaos, confusion, and fear. There is literally a place of absolute peace in Christ that we can find nowhere else! There is not a place on this Earth where He is not right there with you, aware of every intricate part of your life. His love for you is unfathomable! His knowledge of you… indescribable!

Psalm 139 describes it as only the Spirit of the Living God is able!

"O Lord, You have searched me and known me.
You know my sitting down and my rising up;
You understand my thought afar off.
You comprehend my path and my lying down,
And are acquainted with all my ways.
For there is not a word on my tongue,
But behold, O Lord, You know it altogether.

From the Green River to the Lily of the Valley

You have hedged me behind and before,
And laid Your hand upon me.
Such knowledge is too wonderful for me;
It is high, I cannot attain it.
Where can I go from Your Spirit?
Or where can I flee from Your presence?
If I ascend into heaven, You are there;
If I make my bed in hell, behold, You are there.
If I take the wings of the morning,
And dwell in the uttermost parts of the sea,
Even there Your hand shall lead me,
And Your right hand shall hold me.
If I say, "Surely the darkness shall fall on me,"
Even the night shall be light about me;
Indeed, the darkness shall not hide from You,
But the night shines as the day;
The darkness and the light are both alike to You.
For You formed my inward parts;
You covered me in my mother's womb.
I will praise You, for I am fearfully and wonderfully made;
Marvelous are Your works,
And that my soul knows very well.
My frame was not hidden from You,
When I was made in secret,
And skillfully wrought in the lowest parts of the earth.
Your eyes saw my substance, being yet unformed.
And in Your book they all were written,
The days fashioned for me,
When as yet there were none of them.

How precious also are Your thoughts to me, O God!
How great is the sum of them!
If I should count them, they would be more in number than the sand;
When I awake, I am still with You.
Oh, that You would slay the wicked, O God!
Depart from me, therefore, you bloodthirsty men.
For they speak against You wickedly;
Your enemies take Your name in vain.
Do I not hate them, O Lord, who hate You?
And do I not loathe those who rise up against You?
I hate them with perfect hatred;
I count them my enemies.
Search me, O God, and know my heart;
Try me, and know my anxieties;
And see if there is any wicked way in me,
And lead me in the way everlasting. " Psalm 139, NKJV

I challenge you to read this Psalm every day for the next week, even month, if you are able. Journal your thoughts before you read concerning your life and where you are currently, then journal what you hear in your spirit each day until the end. You will be surprised at how your thoughts about yourself and God will change by hiding the Word of God in your heart.

We must be eternally grateful for all He has given us in this life. He owes us nothing, but gave us everything! As I stated earlier, we deserved death, but He took that death upon Himself on the Cross of Calvary and once and for all, defeated death, hell, and the grave for all that will receive Him. That is Good News my friends!!! When you begin to get anxious, fearful, or depressed, go to His Word and find out what He says about what you are going through. When you have thoughts of harming yourself or that you are not worthy to live, seek Him wholeheartedly and He will speak to you! Philippians 4:8 has completely changed my thinking.

"Finally, brethren, whatsoever things are true, whatsoever things are honest, whatsoever things are just, whatsoever things are pure, whatsoever things are lovely, whatsoever things are of good report; if there be any virtue, and if there be any praise, think on these things."

When I am sitting in my chair and I begin to get anxious and my mind is spinning all around, and I think, "Oh my God, I don't have enough money," or "I owe all of this money, how am I going to pay this?" "I am going to be homeless!" I don't know about you, but I can go from 0-90 in two seconds! So, what does He tell me to do, you to do? Think of things that are true! Honest. Just. Pure. Lovely. Of a good report. Take your thoughts off of your current situation, and shift them to the promises of God for your life. Begin to take authority in your life. Speak the power, the authority, and the Blood of Jesus Christ over your life and put the devil under your feet! He has no power or authority in your life! He will flee when put these principles into practice.

"Submit yourselves therefore to God. Resist the devil, and he will flee from you" James 4:7, NKJV.

Finally, I want to share with you probably one of the greatest remedies and prescriptions for getting healed, delivered, and set free from addiction... *serving others (Step 12, Alcoholics Anonymous)*. Even in all of my pain, trauma, and spiraling life, I found that when I began to serve others that were in the streets, prostitutes, drug addicts, the homeless… the forgotten, little by little, my heart, my mind, my soul, and my spirit were healing, as well. When I began feeding the homeless, clothing and supporting women and children, and giving to others what had been given to me in my darkest times, my purpose in this life began to form right before my eyes. It is truly in service where God begins to reveal your gifts, purpose, and identity not only in this life, but in the Kingdom of God. The Kingdom is polar opposite of the world. The world will tell you that others should serve you, but in the Kingdom of God, servanthood is the way of Christ.

"Therefore if there is any consolation in Christ, if any comfort of love, if any fellowship of the Spirit, if any affection and mercy, fulfill my joy by being like-minded, having the same love, being of one accord, of one mind. Let nothing be done through selfish ambition or conceit, but in lowliness of mind let each esteem others better than himself. Let each of you look out not only for his own interests, but also for the interests of others."

"Let this mind be in you which was also in Christ Jesus, who, being in the form of God, did not consider it robbery to be equal with God, but made Himself of no reputation, taking the form of a bondservant, and coming in the likeness of men. And being found in appearance as a man, He humbled Himself and became obedient to the point of death, even the death of the cross" Philippians 2:1-8, NKJV.

If our Lord humbled Himself in the form of a bondservant, how much more should we humble ourselves and serve our fellow man? It is easy to fall into the pity party of life's "unfair" circumstances and want others to acknowledge your pain and suffering, which there is a time for, but there is also a time to grow, to mature, and to come to the other side of your pain, so you can bring someone else out of their pain. This is where you will find your victory! Don't remain in that place of defeat and allow the enemy to steal, kill, and destroy your life. Rise above what happened to you, and allow God to use it for His Glory! I am praying for you. I am cheering for you!

Chapter 14

Wedding Bells

**"So then, they are no longer two but one flesh.
Therefore what God has joined together, let not man separate."
Matthew 19:6, NKJV**

I had been living in my home for about six months with the woman from the Women's house. I knew she was using alcohol and drugs again and I brought it up to my counselor. The counselor had actually been meeting with her, as well. The woman became very manipulative, and I have to say, I knew how to manipulate very well, too, throughout the many years I spent in the streets, so I could easily recognize it when it was being done. Sadly, the reason she was so manipulative is because she believed that drugs and alcohol were her only way to survive. She did not believe that God could heal her, deliver her, and set her free. I had to protect myself and my own recovery; I could not have an alcoholic and drug addict living with me, even though I was deathly afraid to be alone. Well, before I could even approach her to make the decision, she and my counselor came over together and explained that she would be moving out. It was a blessing and a curse all at the same time. I would not have to deal with the alcohol and drugs, but now reality is settling in… I would once again be alone.

The thoughts of how I would take care of myself loomed over me. The thoughts of no one being there with me in case something happened flooded my mind. Toney and I had been in marriage counseling for about a year now, but I did not want to make the wrong decision to marry him simply because I was afraid to be alone. We both still had some serious issues to work out individually before we could make the commitment to marry and live together forever, or was I just afraid to be happy. One day, Toney and I took a drive down to Saltwater Park and he spilled out his heart to me. He said, "Susie, I have been asking you to marry me for six years. I really want to be a pastor and I cannot do that without my helpmate. I really want us to move to the next level, what we have been praying about and what God has prophesied over our lives. Please, consider marrying me. You are by yourself and I really believe now is the time that God wants us to move forward." I had already asked everyone that we knew what their thoughts were and we had been in marriage counseling for a year. I looked up to the heavens and then turned to him and said, "Yes, I will marry you." I loved Toney deeply. I knew that I could never be without him and that we would one day be married, but I also knew that every decision I had made in my life was made with the spirit of fear behind it. I did not want that to be the case anymore. I wanted to break that cycle in my life.

Yes, I was alone. I did not have my biological family in my life because they didn't want anything to do with me. My children were estranged from me at that time because they, too, were working through their own childhood traumas. Though I knew there would be a long road ahead of us working through a lot of our own unhealed places, I knew we had God. I knew that God had brought him into my life. Toney loved God, probably more than I did, so I knew we would be okay. I told him I was too anxious to wait a year to marry him, so I told him, "Let's get married next Saturday!" So, we had a wedding in seven days. He went and got the marriage license, and a friend of mine put the wedding together for us. Pastor Bob married us and it was a cute, sweet, and beautiful wedding. When I look at our wedding pictures, it is obvious that Toney and I were in love with one another and still are to this day.

Toney has been my protector and taught me how to be more humble before the Lord and how to repent and become closer to God. He has taught me the Word of God and how to be a peacemaker. My husband is truly a gift from God and I am eternally grateful to God for bringing him into my life, but there were some things that I needed to learn from the Word of God in how to be a submissive wife. I was not, by any means, a submissive woman. I came from a place of brokenness and abuse. If you hurt me, I was guarding myself and not even thinking about submitting to you in any way. I had a warped idea of what true submission was in God's eyes. It is not about what you are doing to me and my reaction to it; it is about trusting God that He was not going to hurt me or allow someone else to, either. He was going to fight my battles and I had to submit to that truth in my life. I had to learn that in submitting to my husband, I was submitting to the Lord. I was submitting to His love, His direction, His guidance, and His love through Toney. Even if he is wrong, and my God we all are wrong at times, as long as he is doing what he believes is right and walking in God's will, I will follow him and submit to him. If he is outside of God's will, then as his wife, I will definitely communicate my concerns, but I am still in submission to him as my head, and the Lord.

"Wives, submit to your own husbands, as to the Lord. For the husband is the head of the wife even as Christ is the head of the church, his body, and is himself its Savior. Now as the church submits to Christ, so also wives should submit in everything to their husbands" Ephesians 5:22-24, NKJV.

We got married on September 28, 2013, in my home because again, I could not go very far. Toney told me one day, "If you can never drive further than the corner store from our house, I still want to spend the rest of my life with you." He has been a good husband. He has had his own challenges in his life, which I will let him share when he is ready, but he is a good man. What I love the most about him is that he loves God more than he loves anybody or anything. He will lay his life down for Jesus Christ. Today, I am the same woman for God that he is as a man, for the Lord. My husband moved into our home with me and I was so excited. I was truly at peace for probably the first time in my life. We would have little Bible studies in our home and have outside church where we would go out into the streets and share the Gospel. At one point, we did it with megaphones and signs; we were all about trying to build the Kingdom of God. I was still going to *Christ's Church* and he began to go with me. Toney became a member with me and we remained there for about ten years or so.

Marriage was not that easy at first; mind you, we had been courting for six years and not living together. The things you did when you were courting are much different than when you get married and are living in the same home. I did not have the best examples growing up of what a husband was, or even what a wife was truly supposed to be. My father was abusive and completely dysfunctional, my boyfriend who lied to me and took my virginity and then tried to slit my throat with a bottle, then my first husband who was very bipolar, sick, and definitely not walking with the Lord, and then pimps. I had three pimps in my prostitution days. I did not have a very good understanding of what love was supposed to be, relationship, or anything. My mother was abused by my father and was very controlling up until the day he died. He was able to get sober and they had about thirteen years of a better marriage past all of that, but there was still a lot of control in him. I hope and pray that she experienced some sort of joy in marriage in those last years.

Unfortunately, I did not know a lot about good marriages or healthy relationships. I was still seeing Dani for biblical counseling to help me with anxiety, fear, and depression, and we were doing Bible studies on those topics. Elise Fitzpatrick has a Bible study on "Fear & Anxiety," and this helped me out tremendously. I also needed to work on "people pleasing," which was a huge stronghold in my life for a long time. My precious friend and counselor Dani began to walk through the most horrific season in her life, yet she continued to come and help me through my struggles and fear. Eventually, she moved away to Portland, and I had other wonderful counselors to come and support me. I did also have a worldly counselor that did help me get through a lot of my anxiety, but she wanted me to do things dealing with PTSD that really scared me and brought fear into my life, so I ended sessions with her. I went back to *Christ's Church* and there was a woman named Anna, another angel in my life, that agreed to counsel me. I have worked with her for many years, and she has helped me in so many areas of my life. Here are some scriptures Anna taught me to speak to God daily. Even in Anna's own physical issues, she has been a faithful, kind friend that I will always be thankful to God for bringing me.

I am fifty-one years old at this point in my life, and struggling greatly with anxiety and menopause. Toney and I began a Celebrate Recovery class in our home, which was absolutely amazing. We have been doing this now for going on eleven years. I am struggling immensely at this point to go outside, and my counselor Anna would come over every Saturday to my home for counseling sessions, faithfully. I really need the one on one with a woman, especially a woman of God. We started delving down deeper into the issues in my heart. I was working full-time and my business was growing, and it was very stressful. The menopause did not help it at all, because I could not go out of the house. A hysterectomy was out of the question because of my obesity. I was just not feeling great physically, whatsoever.

Anna gave me scriptures to meditate upon and a friend of mine plopped them right in front of my computer one time because I was yelling and having a bad day. The first one stated, *"This is the day the Lord has made, let us rejoice and be glad in it"* (Psalm 118:24, NKJV). Anna asked me a very hard question. She said, "Can you be content right where you are at? Can you be content if you never go two blocks from this house?" I was not sure that I could, but I was willing to trust God. My security in Christ was growing every single day from the Bible studies and the Word of God that was coming forth from our church. The amount of information I was given biblically was absolutely phenomenal. The membership package from *Christ's Church* was like a diamond in the rough when it came to Scripture and theology. That entire training was so enlightening for my Christian walk. My issue was that I thought I knew more than everyone else. My pride kept me from growing as fast as I should have, because I had a lot of life experience, but of course, I did not grow up with biblical knowledge, wisdom, and understanding.

I took to Anna quickly and I would really listen to her, as she was so kind and sweet. She knew the Word of God deeply and would keep me on track when I would fall away. The second scripture was Psalm 51:10, which says, *"Create in me a clean heart, O God, And renew a steadfast spirit within me,"* NKJV.

Finally, Psalm 19:14 (NKJV), which states: *"Let the words of my mouth and the meditation of my heart Be acceptable in Your sight, O Lord, my strength and my Redeemer."* These scriptures began to take root in my heart, and completely transformed my walk with Christ. My adult children are now living with us at this point. I thought I would be ecstatic having them living with me because I could not leave the house, but after three years, it did not work out. My daughter moved out and got her own place. My middle son was coming to see me, but our relationship was still strained because I had given him up for adoption. I had to explain and re-explain often the reasoning behind my decision, and I have always been confident that I did not give him up selfishly. It was probably one of the only unselfish acts I ever made in my entire life. I truly believed in my heart of hearts that I was giving him a better life that he so desperately needed, based upon the trauma he incurred in the early part of his childhood, while I was leaving his father.

Prayerfully, he has now admitted in his middle age that his adoptive parents did give him a better life and that He forgives me. I have always loved all my children and although I wasn't the best mother, my heart wanted to be. I can say that I have been a good mother for the last twenty-five years and I am glad I have been able to make living amends to my children.

I never shut the door on him and I dealt with whatever he threw at me; I never stopped loving him. I never stopped pursuing him and letting him know I was his mother. My eldest son lived near me and came over to help me clean and helped take care of me for a little while. It became apparent to him that he needed to get away and do something different with his life. I was enabling him because I knew I needed him, but it was not healthy nor was it fair to him. He moved to Arizona, which was extremely hard for me. He had a girlfriend that had a beautiful little baby that really became our grandchild even though she was not biologically. Eventually, she took her away from us, which devastated us. Things were not going great in my marriage and we started marriage counseling. Times were getting a little hard for me. Anna still came like clockwork every Saturday and I still had the Celebrate Recovery program on Tuesday nights. I was no longer able to get out to get to church, but I was still watching it on T.V. We also had a Life Group in our home for about a year, which helped a lot because I was able to connect with other Believers.

If your church does not have a Life Group, search out to see where you may find one. It was such an amazing way to stay in touch with people and remain accountable in my walk with God. In 2018, God was about to take us to another level in ministry. A young lady I had ministered to for many years and her two kids moved in with us to help me because I needed housekeeping and other help. I was still working full-time as a self-employed business owner, sometimes 12-13 hours a day. I was taking care of my husband. He was working as a doorman at a local familiar restaurant in the area and I needed additional help. Unfortunately, she did not have good intentions toward us at all. She began stealing from us on a credit card in the range of about $10,000.00. She was apparently relapsing and I had no clue whatsoever. My friend

Catherine would come and stay overnight with me and help me. I was feeling very overwhelmed and just struggling tremendously. She would come and stay for weeks at a time, and we would just have so much fun. She would bring her puppies with her and was just a real good friend to me when I needed her the most. Toney and I loved her so very much, she was our Seahawks partner and we would sit and watch the games together.

God was ramping us up for the next level and it was becoming more apparent to us very quickly. In October of 2019, Toney acquired Ketoacidosis with sepsis and was extremely sick one night. Another friend was staying with us and this young lady and her two kids were still with us, at that point. Toney was making a real weird noise in his lungs, so I called 911 and they arrived quickly. His blood pressure was down in the 60s and we were losing him. They could not get him from off the floor, so I stood up and began laying my hands on all of the paramedics and firefighters in my home in the name of JESUS CHRIST and all of a sudden, his blood pressure shot up to around 98. They were able to get him up on the gurney, and they put him in the ambulance; he had a really bad seizure and then he coded at the hospital. They rushed him onto a dialysis machine and began emergency resuscitation to keep him alive. The doctor called me and said to me, "Mrs. Bates, I am really sorry but you need to bring your family. Your husband's kidney has failed, his heart and lungs are failing, and he likely is not going to make it."

I told the doctor that he did not know my God, that I was not going to bring my family to the hospital, that I was going to ask people to pray, and that my husband was going to come home. I had about three people working for me that day and one lady named Lindsey jumped up out of her chair because I was crying in my office. I knew I couldn't go and be with him because I could not leave my home. She told me she used to be a paramedic and that she would go and sit with him every day and be my eyes and ears. She told me she would bring a laptop so I could talk to him through Zoom. I went on Facebook to ask all of my friends to pray for him and thousands began to pray for my husband.

I had been grumbling about him for about the last five months before this happened. Things were not going good for us at this time. I did not know he was getting sick, and I was just not in a good place. I could not kneel down on my knees due to my obesity, so I kneeled over my bed and said, "Lord, I apologize for complaining about my husband. Can you please save his life? I cannot see going through this life and fulfilling this ministry You have given us without him." I told Him, "Help me God, I am afraid." Immediately, I felt His peace come over me and I knew Toney was going to be okay and that he was going to come home. No one told me this, but I just knew in my spirit that it was true. I called the nurse that night and she said, "Susan, there is not a huge change, but his numbers are getting better." She said we were not talking about dying now, but about his quality of life. We didn't know if he was going to be on dialysis forever or what he was going to look like when he did come home.

I was so grateful that he was just coming home. My sister is a nurse and was so kind to call the doctor and speak with him to find out what was really wrong with him and causing these issues. They put him in an induced coma and I would call him and pray with him and sing to him, and the young lady that worked for me was sitting with him daily to encourage him. God brought another angel into my life to help me. It is hard to lose what stability you thought you had in a family. As I have stated before, you can pick your sin, but you cannot pick your consequences. I went almost an entire lifetime without the blessing of my family. I do not blame them; I blame myself. I would sit in my chair in my living room that had a view of the moon. I would sit there every night and pray and ask God to continue to heal Toney and to forgive me for how I talked to him. I would say, "Father, just bring my husband home, so we can do Your will."

The devil was trying to destroy our family through that young lady that was robbing us. Her mother was coming and robbing us, as well. She was trying to entice things and trying to start things between me and my husband. The wrong people were in our home, but the power of God was in our home, as well, and He was not going to allow it. Toney was in critical care ICU and his numbers were getting better every day, but he was still in a coma on a breathing tube. I continued to pray and would not listen to anything people were saying around me that did not line up with the Word of God. There were even pastors that would come over and say that things were not looking good for Toney. They were telling me to prepare myself for him to pass away. A neighbor came over and told me the very same thing. I told both of them that I was going to stand by faith and not by sight. I told them I was going to trust in the God that I had believed in all these years, and I was going to watch Him create a miracle in my husband's life.

Anna was still coming to see me and she was my lifeline to the truth of God's Word. She was just a good woman and a good friend. We were two weeks into him being in the ICU and they were thinking of taking him off the breathing tube. His numbers were getting better and he was beginning to respond. My sweet friend Lindsay and her husband went to the hospital with a JESUS IS GOD t-shirt at 3 o'clock in the morning and sat with Toney for twelve hours while the doctors tried to get the breathing tube out of his throat. Toney was rejecting it and did not want to let it go. Finally, Anna sat with me and we prayed and we believed, and twelve hours later, Toney came out of his coma. His first words were: GOD, MIRACLE, JESUS. For those words to come out of his mouth right out of a coma, I knew the Holy Spirit was speaking through him and letting me know I could trust Him. He was letting me know through Toney's experience that was He was increasing and building my faith to a greater place than it had ever been in my entire life. Although it was a horrific and horrible time, I know that God had brought Toney back because He had a huge plan for our lives.

Toney finally gets out of the hospital and this girl and her two children were still living with us and her mother was still coming around and causing confusion. It all began to fall apart because she was leaving and going to see pimps and leaving her children with us. She was being paid to help me, but was never around to carry out those responsibilities. We knew it was time to let her go, but we had no idea who would be helping us next. I was now faced with the reality that God was trying to heal me of my anxiety and fear that had plagued me all of my life. I was now being thrust into the face of God and being held accountable to trust Him, and Him alone. Out of all the fears in my life, this may very well have been the absolute greatest fear of all. Not that I was scared of Him, but I now had to actually face the roots of that fear and allow HIM to heal me and deliver me.

Chapter 15

Biblical Counseling

"Where there is no counsel, the people fall;
But in the multitude of counselors there is safety."
Proverbs 11:14, NKJV

God had finally gotten me to that infamous *crossroad* we all face in our lives at some point. There was a man that Toney and I were introduced to from another program, along with his wife, that came to visit us at our home. He spoke about wanting to be a pastor and desiring to open up his own housing program, where he said he felt he heard the Lord say that He healed Toney's body because he was supposed to be ordained to serve God and help in this program. We began to pray with this couple and seek God for His voice and His wisdom. In the meantime, we began to build our church behind our home with a program called "Praisealleujah". Our church was completed in May of 2020, a cute little 1000sq.ft. church in the back of one of our houses. This man came to work for Toney and me in our business and began his church within our church. We decided that we were going to help him with what God had blessed our family with, which is always God's heart. We birthed the ministry and began our church where this man preached and Toney was ordained underneath of his covering.

Toney had been promised this under several different churches previously, but it never came to fruition. They overlooked his gifts and his calling due to his past failures. It just was simply not God's timing in that season. The pastor of the church we birthed preached in the church for about a year and promised that after the first year, he would ordain Toney into the ministry as a pastor, but it never happened. Toney was heartbroken. All that he has ever wanted to do since he was six years old was to be a pastor and preach God's Word. This was his heart. Well, time went on and we continued to have church, Bible Studies, and all kinds of meetings every night of the week. We had, at this point, let the young lady and her two kids go from our home because of her stealing from us. We chose not to prosecute her because she was already doing so with the lifestyle she had chosen to live. God told us to let it go and to trust Him to restore, and He absolutely did, above and beyond all we could have ever asked or thought to ask.

"Now all glory to God, who is able, through his mighty power at work within us, to accomplish infinitely more than we might ask or think" Ephesians 3:20, NLT.

We are praying and believing God for restoration in her life. The pastor and his wife were now with us and the ministry was finally taking off, and then in 2020, Covid hit the world. It was shocking, at first, but we did not allow it to stop the Gospel from going forth; we continued with church and our Bible studies. We did contract Covid twice, but we made it through and did not know anyone that died except and 80-year-old man that had many underlying issues where he was not able to fight it with his immune system. After the year of this pastor not following through with his promise to ordain Toney, and many other issues that were beginning to surface, including theological doctrines and heresy that we could not come into agreement with, as well as bringing "prophets" that were still using drugs, Toney had to ask him to leave.

We took a few weeks break from the ministry, seeking the Lord for what was to be next because we needed a pastor and Toney had not yet been ordained. We knew wholeheartedly that it is God who ordains and that God had called Toney many years prior through his heart's desire to shepherd God's people. We were at a Celebrate Recovery meeting one night and an elder friend of mine contacted me and told me that the elders had prayed and had a meeting and they believed the Lord was telling them to ordain Toney as a pastor. She stated that Toney had been overlooked too many times, and that God said it was time. I immediately contacted our current pastor as *Christ's Church*, Pastor Jeff, and explained to him that the elders of this church were going to ordain Toney as a pastor and asked how he felt about it. He was happy and said he was all for it, but that he could not be there because he would be traveling to Florida. We were so happy for his blessing over Toney.

"Unless the Lord builds the house, They labor in vain who build it" Psalm 127:1, NKJV.

I was ecstatic and so excited to share the wonderful news with Toney that he was going to be ordained as a pastor. We knew it was God building His Church, because we did not move ahead of Him and we submitted ourselves underneath of the pastor, and even when he refused to ordain Toney, we did not rebel and simply step out on our own. We waited, prayed earnestly, sought out counsel, continued to serve, and

God Himself "saw" it all. He is El Roi, the God who sees! We knew it was Him because we did not seek it out, but He moved upon the hearts of the elders of the Church on Toney's, His servant, heart.

Sitting in that Celebrate Recovery meeting with my precious husband, I looked over at him and said, "Tone, the elders, Pastor Russ, Steph, and Brad, they want to ordain you." He looked at me and said, "What?" I repeated to him that they wanted to ordain him, and he just began crying. He put his hands over his face with tears flowing, thanking God for His faithfulness. I later emailed Steph and asked when they would be available for the ordination and began to prepare for the meeting with the elders. On August 1, 2021, Toney was ordained as pastor of *Jesus is God Ministry*. We had our sign made and put it up and began having church again. We were so excited. We opened up our house as a discipleship home and began moving men into the house. We moved one woman into the apartment on the side of the house, as she was going to be the caregiver for the elderly men in the program in their 70s and 80s.

The house was beginning to fill up and I began having Women's Conferences, and was truly excited about ministry. My husband began to grow exponentially as an amazing pastor and leader. We knew God was building HIS Church. After the first year of ministry at *Jesus is God Ministry*, we purchased and remodeled a second house, and by December of 2022, we signed the lease on the third house, which is our Women's house. I have been privileged to minister to these precious women, while Toney ministers and walks alongside of the men in the Men's houses. The vision and prophecy that was prophesied over our lives years earlier was now being birthed. God has blessed us and done so much through us for this community. We are seeking God daily for

His will and what He desires to do next in and through us. We are reaching out to agencies and organizations to partner with us to continue the work of the Kingdom.

"What man of you, having a hundred sheep, if he loses one of them, does not leave the ninety-nine in the wilderness, and go after the one which is lost until he finds it?" Luke 15:4, NKJV.

This is our heart. We believe in quality, not quantity. We pray that we are making sure that the people God is bringing us, that we are taking care of their souls. For the last three years, my husband has dressed up in his Jesus is God t-shirt and gone out into the streets of Kent, Des Moines, Federal Way, and Auburn and shared the Gospel with over four thousand people. Of that four thousand, around one thousand of these people have received treatment. Many of the others are still around here and there, familiar faces that we have ministered to over the years.

Toney goes out every single day, Monday through Friday, and he shares the Gospel, bringing bibles, sack lunches, and hygiene items with a group of people from our church to share the love of God. When you are completely broken and living on a street corner, in a bush, in a motel, or in a place that is certainly not at your best, the love of God is the only thing that can touch your heart at that point. You feel thrown away by the world and that your family doesn't want you anymore. Maybe you didn't have a family, and you feel all alone. This is God's opportune moment to reconcile with you to let you know that if there is no one else on this Earth that is thinking about you, or mindful of you, that He is... and always will.

God wants everyone! I know that is an entirely separate topic of election, but I am not here to debate theology. I am here to tell you what I have experienced on those very streets when I lived on them, and now, when we go back and minister to others the love of Jesus Christ, the Triune God, Father, Son, and Holy Spirit. He is so full of love, grace, and mercy, and He desires that not one is lost.

"Even so it is not the will of your Father who is in heaven that one of these little ones should perish" Matthew 18:14, NKJV.

Chapter 16

The Lily of the Valley

"I am the rose of Sharon, And the lily of the valleys."
Song of Solomon 2:1

I cannot even begin to express without great tears where He has brought me from, and as I swallow those tears right now, I want to share the ending, or shall I say *the beginning* of my new life in Christ. Everything you have heard in my story, in my life, this is what Jesus did for me. He offered me great mercy and grace, and did not allow me to die in those streets. He sheltered me from domestic violence, violent offenders, sick and demonic people, pimps, and yes, even a serial killer. I should have been dead in those streets as a prostitute, an alcoholic, and a drug addict, but He saw fit to save my life. Why? Because He had a greater purpose for me.

I could not fathom or understand why He chose to save me, while many other drug addicts and prostitutes did not make it off those streets alive, including the beautiful women I knew that were murdered by Gary Ridgway, the Green River Killer. Why was I still here? Well, it was not, and is not, my place to question God. He is God, and His plans are greater than we could ever think or imagine.

"For My thoughts are not your thoughts, Nor are your ways My ways," says the Lord. "For as the heavens are higher than the earth, So are My ways higher than your ways, And My thoughts than your thoughts" Isaiah 55:8-9, NKJV.

I just allowed God to use me, but I have fought every step of the way; I had a lot of fear, anxiety, depression, and hopelessness, but He walked with me every step of the way! God restored every single one of those things in my life, or has completely removed them! It is an absolute miracle, because I did not take any medication whatsoever for any of these issues, not that I am against medication, but for me, Holy Spirit performed these miracles in my life. Not only that, but my finances were completely restored after filing bankruptcy twice in my life, and was on my way to a third when my mother passed away. But God said, "NO!" I will restore you! He led me to a wonderful company to work where I made very good money. They also allowed me to become a contractor where I could work for others to increase my income, so we could continue to do the work of the ministry, building the Kingdom of God.

We don't make money to go on extravagant trips to France or to go on long cruises in the Caribbean; we make money to support and finance the Kingdom of God: helping the poor, feeding the homeless, taking care of the widows and the orphans, helping the alcoholics and drug addicts get treatment, supporting the prostitutes trying to get away from pimps and off the streets, and supporting single mothers and ex-convicts, those thrown away by the world.

From the Green River to the Lily of the Valley

"If someone has enough money to live well and sees a brother or sister in need but shows no compassion—how can God's love be in that person?" 1 John 3:17, NLT.

All of the assets we own are for the Kingdom of God, our home, our ministry houses, our ministry, our business, our cars, all material things we possess, and even our lives, are not our own. We have given up everything for the Kingdom and laid down our lives for Jesus Christ. We love God so much, and He has brought us both out of some of the darkest places in this world. We have vowed to serve Him and humanity for the rest of our lives. Every breathing second that He gives us on this side of eternity, we will use it for His glory. I now see differently, hear differently, and live differently. I am getting "old" in this natural body and whether my joints are hurting, or I did not sleep well, or my hormones are out of whack, I wake up every morning simply rejoicing because He loves me so very much and has still given me breath in my body to do His will in the Earth.

I want to encourage you that as you repent and receive Jesus Christ as your Lord and Savior, surrender and submit your life to serving Him and building His Kingdom, He will bless you, redeem you, restore you, and reconcile you for His great purposes. He will go above and beyond to heal you, deliver you, and set you free from any and all past traumas, abuses, and torment you may have faced in your childhood, teenage years, or even adulthood. He will reconcile relationships, including estranged family members and even bring His best into your life. Trust me, He did it for me!

God blessed me with my wonderful husband, Toney. He is a godly man who loves me, cares for me, and supports me; he is my best friend, my leader, my spiritual counselor, and yes, my pastor. After all those years of abusive men that I allowed into my life, God finally brought the man HE chose to be my husband into my life. He is truly a man after his Father's heart. He loves me as Christ loves the Church and has laid down his life for the Kingdom of God. I am truly a blessed woman and I do not take it, or him, for granted. God saved his life and gave me back my husband, for which I am eternally grateful.

God gave me back my little boy that I gave up for adoption, Eric. Well, he is not a little boy anymore, but I lost so many years with him that he still feels like that "little boy" to me. Two years ago, he finally forgave me for giving him up, and it was truly a cleansing of my soul because I had waited so many years to hear those words out of his mouth and from his heart. He calls me "Momma," and he is so blessed to have two mommas, two dads, lots of cousins, his biological brothers and sisters, and non-biological, which are still his siblings. He is a blessed young man and he gave me two beautiful grandchildren whom I love dearly. We are building a beautiful relationship and I am so very proud of the man he has become. His aunt and uncle raised him so well, and for that, I am eternally grateful.

God also restored my relationship with my oldest son, Elliot. He forgave me this year (2023) and God allowed us to reconcile. He is back in church and married, living his life the very best way he can. I am so extremely proud of him. When I gave birth to him, I was a prostitute and coming off drugs and alcohol. I know without a shadow of a doubt that God gave me Elliot to save my life. I may not even be here today if my precious son did not come into this world. I love my son with all of my heart. He brings me great joy and I am so thankful that God has kept him and my other children. They endured a lot during the time of me battling through my own past hurts and traumas, trying to find my way through life. I made some extremely bad choices and because of that, they suffered tremendously, but God is faithful!

My next blessing is my daughter, Elyse. I love her so very much. Her brother used to say that she was my "princess". She was always my baby girl, and she is God's princess to this day. She believes in Jesus and believes in God. Elyse is a phenomenal young woman and mother. She is a teacher and works extremely hard to make sure she is active in her child's life. I am so very proud of her. Our relationship was estranged for a very long time, but I understand that each of us has to go through our own process in life. I have to trust God that she is His child, and He will heal whatever needs to heal within her for His glory. Her precious baby has brought us back together and she now knows, as a mother, how it feels to look in her precious baby's face, as I did in hers, and know what true love feels like. I am so thankful for the reconciliation.

Probably one of the greatest reconciliations that I never thought I would see this side of Heaven was reconciling with all four of my sisters. I spent my entire life without a family because of my bad decisions and their inability to cope with my chaotic life. People say that family is supposed to stick together, but that is actually not true. In Matthew 18, it speaks of the process of dealing with a brother (sister) that is sinning. We are to go to them first and try to reach them. If they will not hear us, we bring one or more witnesses with us to persuade them of their sin. If they still refuse to hear, then we are to bring in the elders, and if they reject the elders, we are pretty much told to treat them as the heathen. I was not listening to anyone! I was falling into holes left and right due to my rebellion, my sin. I was not living right until my latter thirties. It was extremely hard for my sisters to trust me. I can completely understand why they separated themselves from me.

Right after my 60th birthday last year, my daughter had her baby shower and invited my sisters. They came up from Portland and I was so excited and nervous, all at the same time. Two of them came, my twin sisters, and I was waiting like a twelve year old little girl on my scooter that I ride around in due to my physical disability. When they got out of the car, I wanted to show them around and show them all that God was doing and had done in my life. I was able to ask one of my sisters for forgiveness, something I had wanted to do for over thirty years and she forgave me. The other sister and I had reconciled a few years earlier and she had forgiven me. My baby sister was not able to come, but she also had forgiven me. I reached out to her on social media and asked for forgiveness, and she told me, "Susie, I forgave you a long time ago." My heart was extremely full. My eldest sister and I had developed a relationship again around fifteen years ago, so that was truly a blessing in my life.

I know that God is doing amazing things in all of my sisters' lives. Being reconciled to my family was a huge relief, and even healing in my life. I don't get to see them often as I am homebound, but I pray we will be able to get to spend some holidays together. I will try my best to make that happen. As I have "cleaned my side of the street," and sought forgiveness and made amends with my sisters and my children, I know God will do the rest. I have done my very best to be a living amends by following the Cross of Jesus Christ. I don't care how far you have fallen down the scales of life; there is ALWAYS hope and restoration by the Cross and Blood of Jesus Christ! God is a BIG GOD! He created this world before we even arrived. He spoke it into existence. He didn't need us, He chose us. He lives within us. When we come to know this truth intimately, and stop listening to the lies the devil is telling us, or that we are telling ourselves, and allow God to restore our hearts and our minds, then we can truly do ALL things through Christ!

"I can do all things through Christ who strengthens me" Philippians 4:13, NKJV.

I am so extremely grateful to God! I will spend every second of every day for the rest of my life serving Him until I see Him on the clouds! I will get to enter glory in my new body, free from sickness and pain. I will get to see my mom and my dad, my aunts and uncles, and my grandparents, but more importantly, I will Him as He is and spend eternity serving and worshipping my Heavenly Father! What an exciting future to look forward to for those that surrender their lives unto Him, those that become born-again through Jesus Christ, our Lord and Savior.

I know I have used it throughout this book, as it is near and dear to my heart, but I will leave you again with the scripture that literally saved my life, both physically and spiritually,

"For I know the thoughts that I think toward you, says the Lord, thoughts of peace and not of evil, to give you a future and a hope. Then you will call upon Me and go and pray to Me, and I will listen to you. And you will seek Me and find Me, when you search for Me with all your heart" Jeremiah 29:11-13, NKJV.

God is our RESTORER!!! I pray that as you close the pages of this book, you will begin to open the pages of a new book in your life. If you have never accepted Jesus Christ as your personal Savior, the Gospel, the Good News, is available right now for you. We all have sinned and fallen short of the glory of God. We were born into a sinful world due to the fall of mankind. Without Jesus's sacrifice on the Cross, there would be no hope for any one of us. We do not have to work for God's love, He gave it to us for free! All He asks is that you believe and receive, to confess with your mouth that Jesus Christ is Lord and believe that God raised Him from the dead as atonement for your sin. Jesus is the Way, the Truth and the Life, no man can come to the Father except by Him. He did not come into this world to condemn it, but to save it… to save you!

Will you believe Him today? Will you receive Him into your life?

If so, pray this prayer with me:

In the name of Jesus, I come to You right now Lord and I thank You for being the God of all Creation. The Godhead three and one. I believe with the faith of a mustard seed that You are God. I ask You to forgive me of all my sins, all the mistakes I have made, my horrible thoughts and bad behavior, and all those that I have hurt and harmed in my life. Your Word says that You forgive us to the uttermost and that You take our sin and throw it into the sea of forgetfulness as far as the east is from the west. I thank You, Lord. I invite You into my heart, Father. You are not a controlling God; You do not force Yourself on anyone. You desire that we come to You willingly, with our whole hearts. Make me new, Lord. Transform me. Sanctify me. Create in me a clean heart, and renew a right spirit within me. Use me for the betterment of Your Kingdom. I will serve You however You choose to use me, and I will love You all the days of my life. In Jesus' name, Amen.

If you received Jesus into your heart today, and would like more information on how to grow in Christ and to get connected to a Bible believing fellowship of believers, feel free to email me at info@JesusisGodMinistry.com. It would be my honor to help you find a church in your area, and help you get plugged into a Bible teaching, Holy Spirit filled gathering that will help you restore, repair, and re-create your life for His glory.

We all need one another. I love you and I thank you for listening to my story. God loves you more than anyone ever can. He is truly the *Lily of the Valley*!

"I am the Rose of Sharon, And the Lily of the Valleys. Like a lily among thorns, So is my love among the daughters."
Song of Solomon 2:1-2, NKJV

Meet the Author

My name at birth was Susan Patricia Elizabeth Brady, I was born in Portland, Oregon at Emanuel Hospital on August 1, 1962. I have six siblings who range in ages thirteen years my senior and three years beneath me. I had a traumatic childhood and tragic adult life. I found my way with the saving Grace of Jesus Christ.

After salvation, I began to learn how to trust God with the faith of a mustard seed. His promises have all come true in my life. Matthew 6:33 says, *"But seek ye first the kingdom of God, and his righteousness; and all these things shall be added unto you."* He has prospered me, He has healed me, He has restored me, and He has given me a future and hope. Jeremiah 29:11 says, *"For I know the plans I have for you,"* declares the Lord, *"plans to prosper you and not to harm you, plans to give you hope and a future."*

I married in 1987 to Perry Manns and I never changed my name due to honoring my children after the divorce. I married again in 2013 to my current husband, Toney Bates, and so my name is Susie Manns-Bates. God has blessed me with three amazing children and three beautiful grandchildren who are my angels.

I spend my life working so I can give back in ministry to those suffering from the same things I suffered. God makes provisions and a way for me and my husband to do HIS will even when we are still recovering from our past lifestyles.

I will spend the rest of my life serving HIM for HIS Glory and my Good.

Made in the USA
Columbia, SC
31 October 2023